D1096613

THE RED MOTHER ™

VOLUME THREE

Published by

BOOM! ™
STUDIOS

THE RED MOTHER Volume Three, April 2021. Published by BOOM! Studios, a division of Boom Entertainment, Inc. The Red Mother is ™ & © 2021 Jeremy Haun. Originally published in single magazine form as THE RED MOTHER No. 9-12. ™ & © 2020, 2021 Jeremy Haun. All rights reserved. BOOM! Studios™ and the BOOM! Studios logo are trademarks of Boom Entertainment, Inc., registered in various countries and categories. All characters, events, and institutions depicted herein are fictional. Any similarity between any of the names, characters, persons, events, and/or institutions in this publication to actual names, characters, and persons, whether living or dead, events, and/or institutions is unintended and purely coincidental. BOOM! Studios does not read or accept unsolicited submissions of ideas, stories, or artwork.

BOOM! Studios, 5670 Wilshire Boulevard, Suite 400, Los Angeles, CA, 90036-5679. Printed in China. First Printing.

ISBN: 978-1-68415-674-0, eISBN: 978-1-64668-159-4

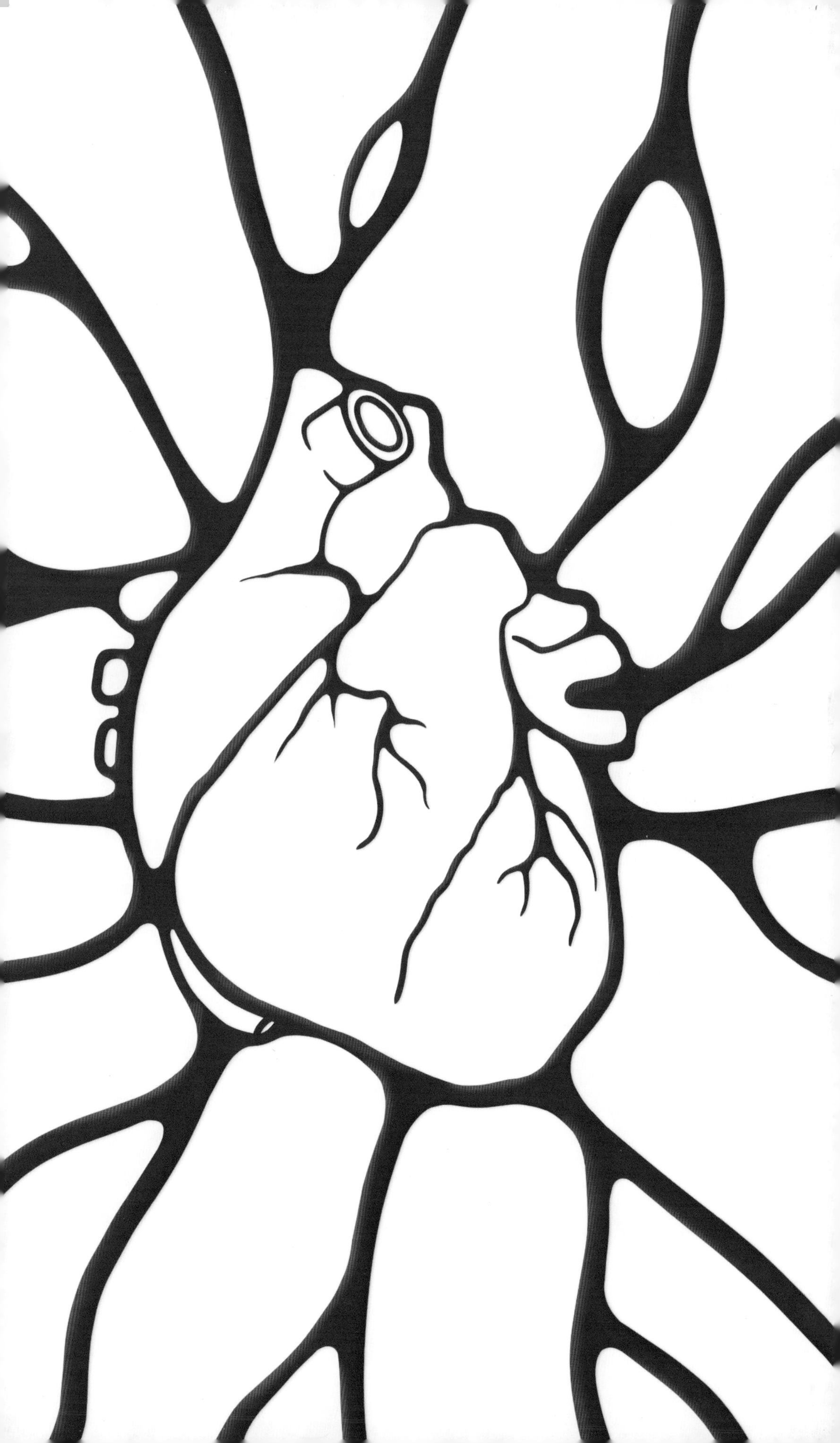

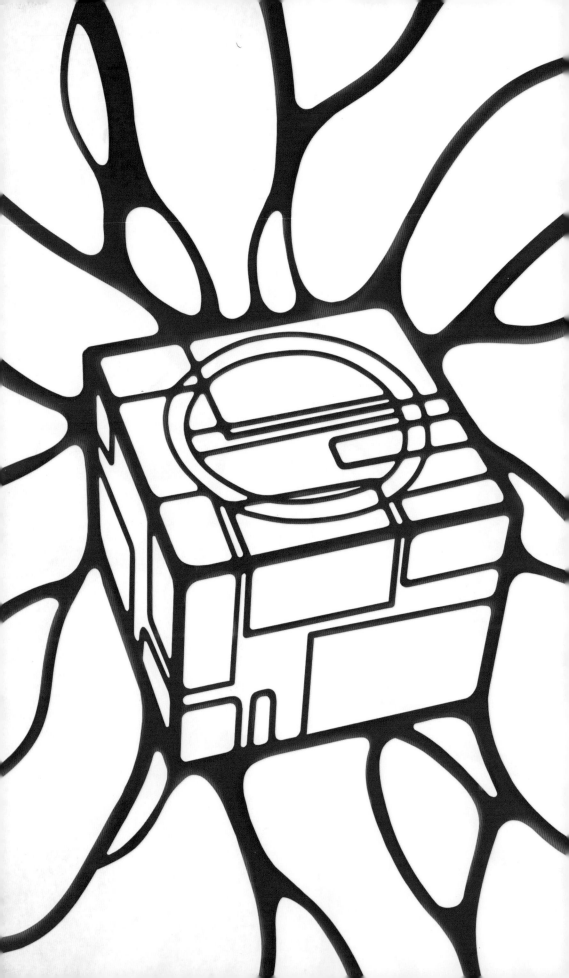

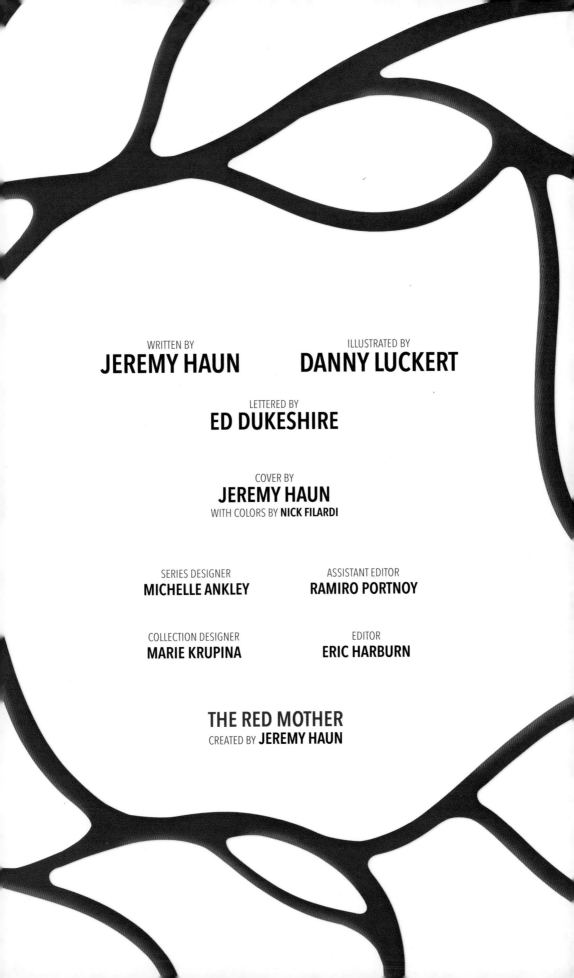

WRITTEN BY
JEREMY HAUN

ILLUSTRATED BY
DANNY LUCKERT

LETTERED BY
ED DUKESHIRE

COVER BY
JEREMY HAUN
WITH COLORS BY **NICK FILARDI**

SERIES DESIGNER
MICHELLE ANKLEY

ASSISTANT EDITOR
RAMIRO PORTNOY

COLLECTION DESIGNER
MARIE KRUPINA

EDITOR
ERIC HARBURN

THE RED MOTHER
CREATED BY **JEREMY HAUN**

CHAPTER
NINE

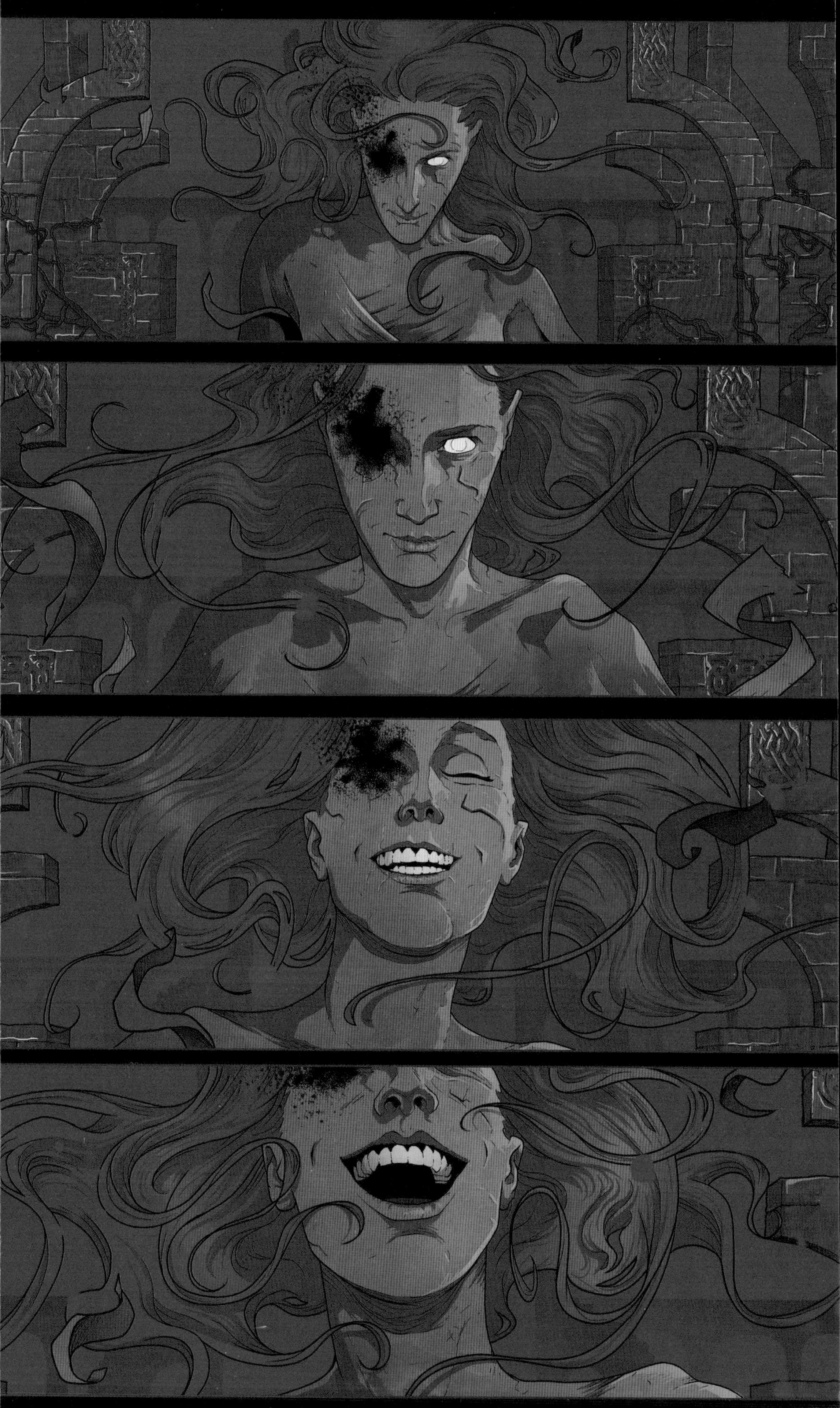

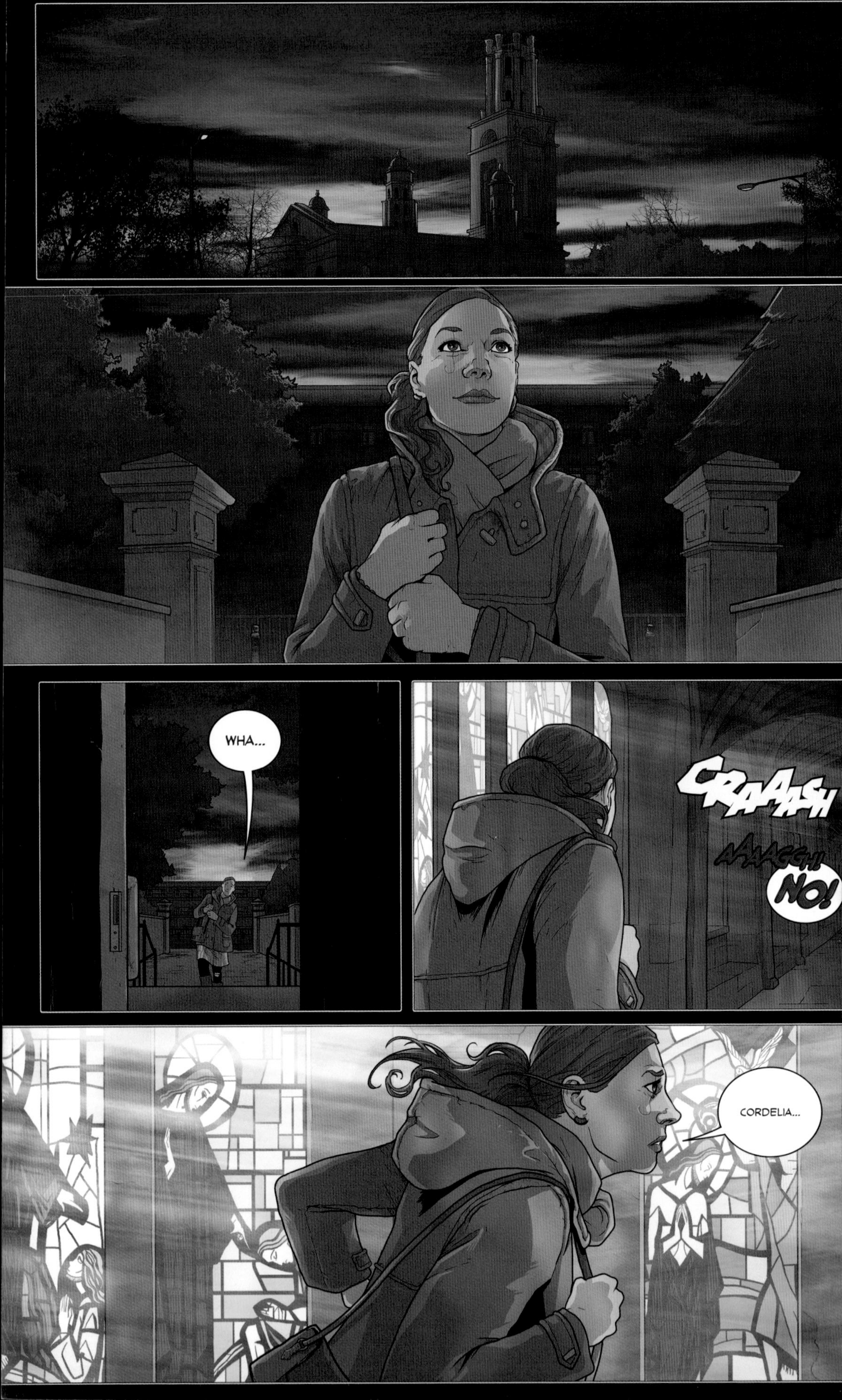
WHA...
CRAAAASH
AAAAGGH!
NO!
CORDELIA...

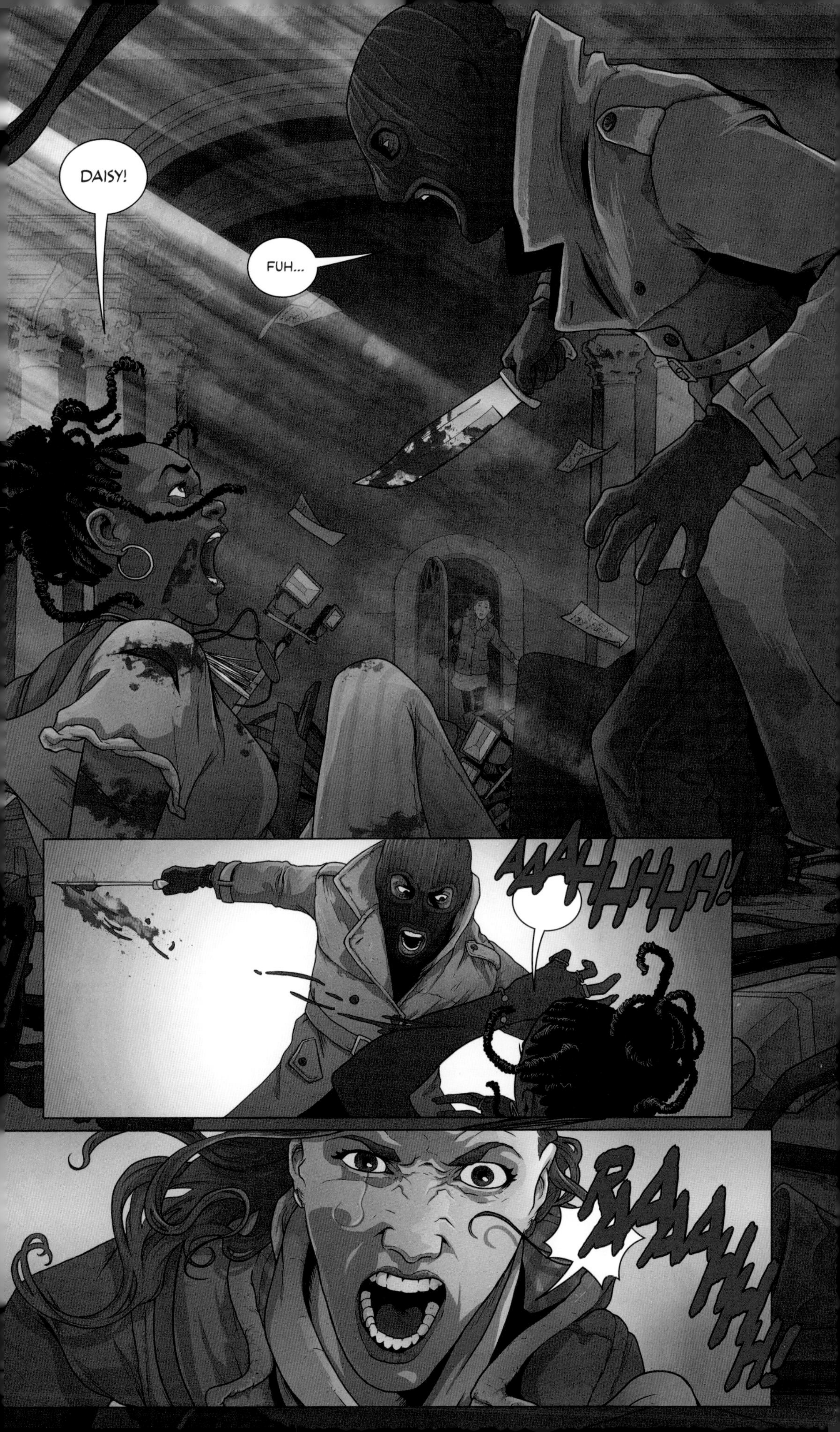
DAISY!
FUH...
AAAHHHHH!
RAAAHHH!

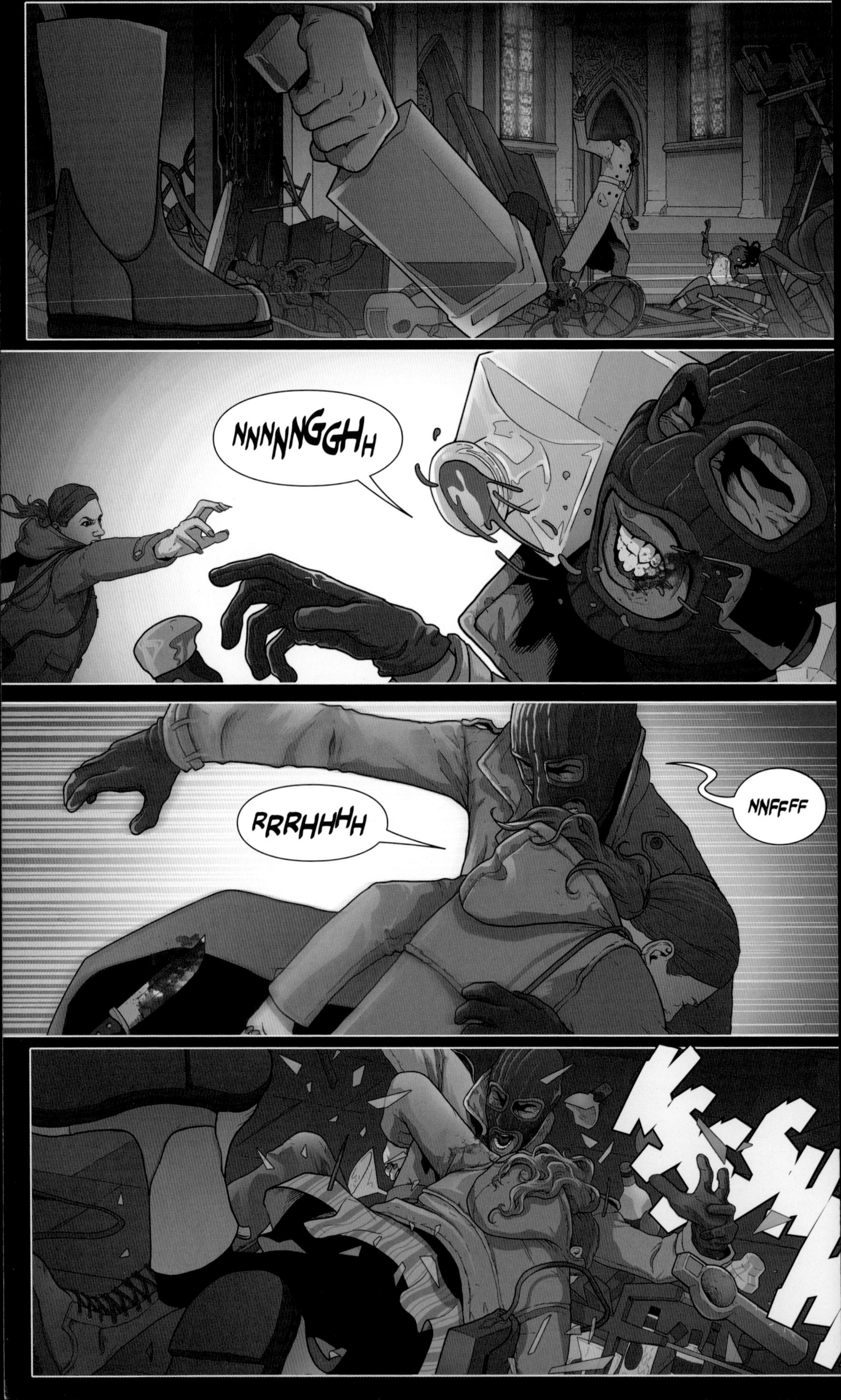
NNNNNGGHH
RRRHHHH
NNFFFF
K-SHH

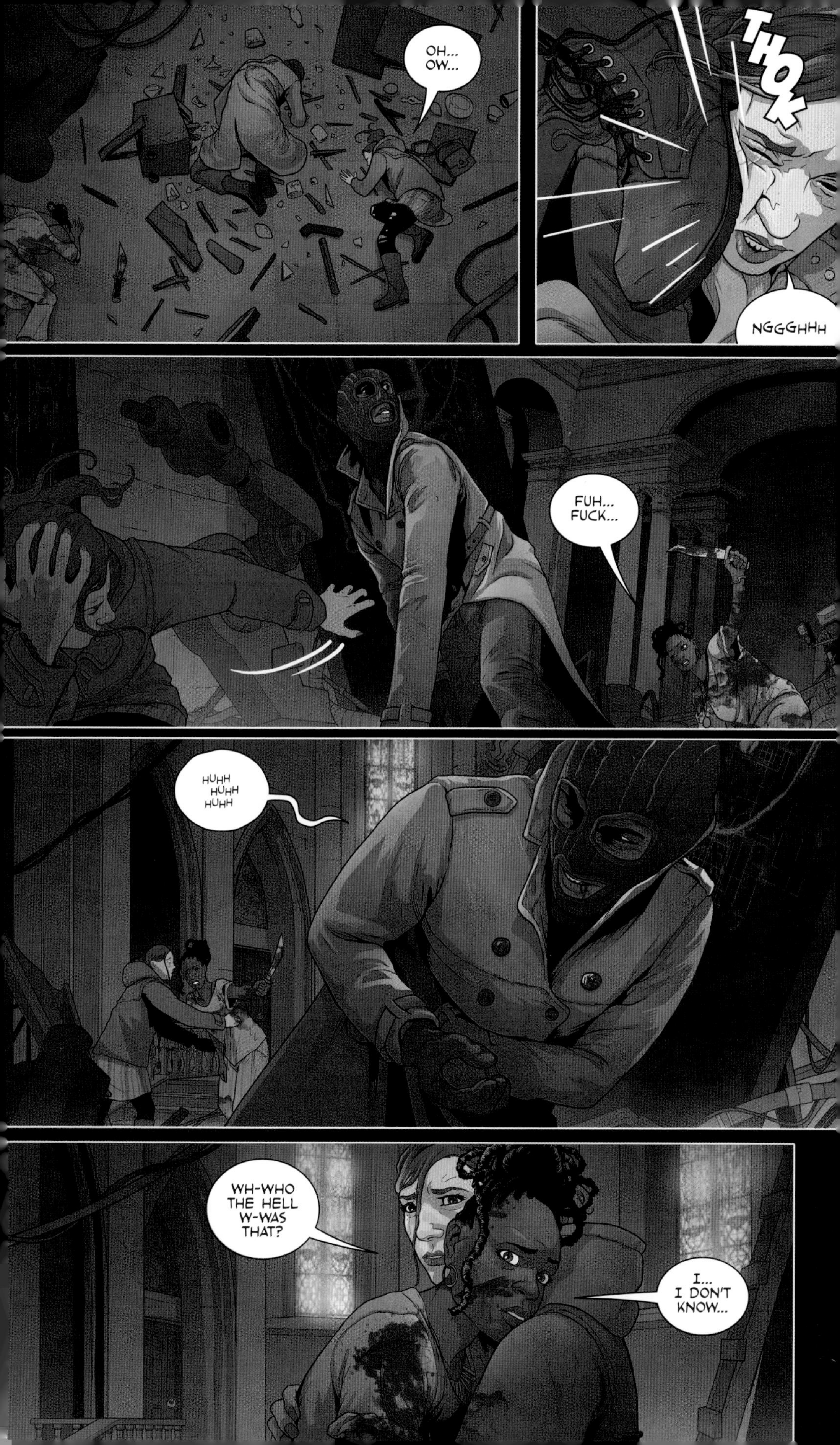
OH... OW...
THOK
NGGGHHH
FUH... FUCK...
HUHH HUHH HUHH
WH-WHO THE HELL W-WAS THAT?
I... I DON'T KNOW...

THE RED MOTHER

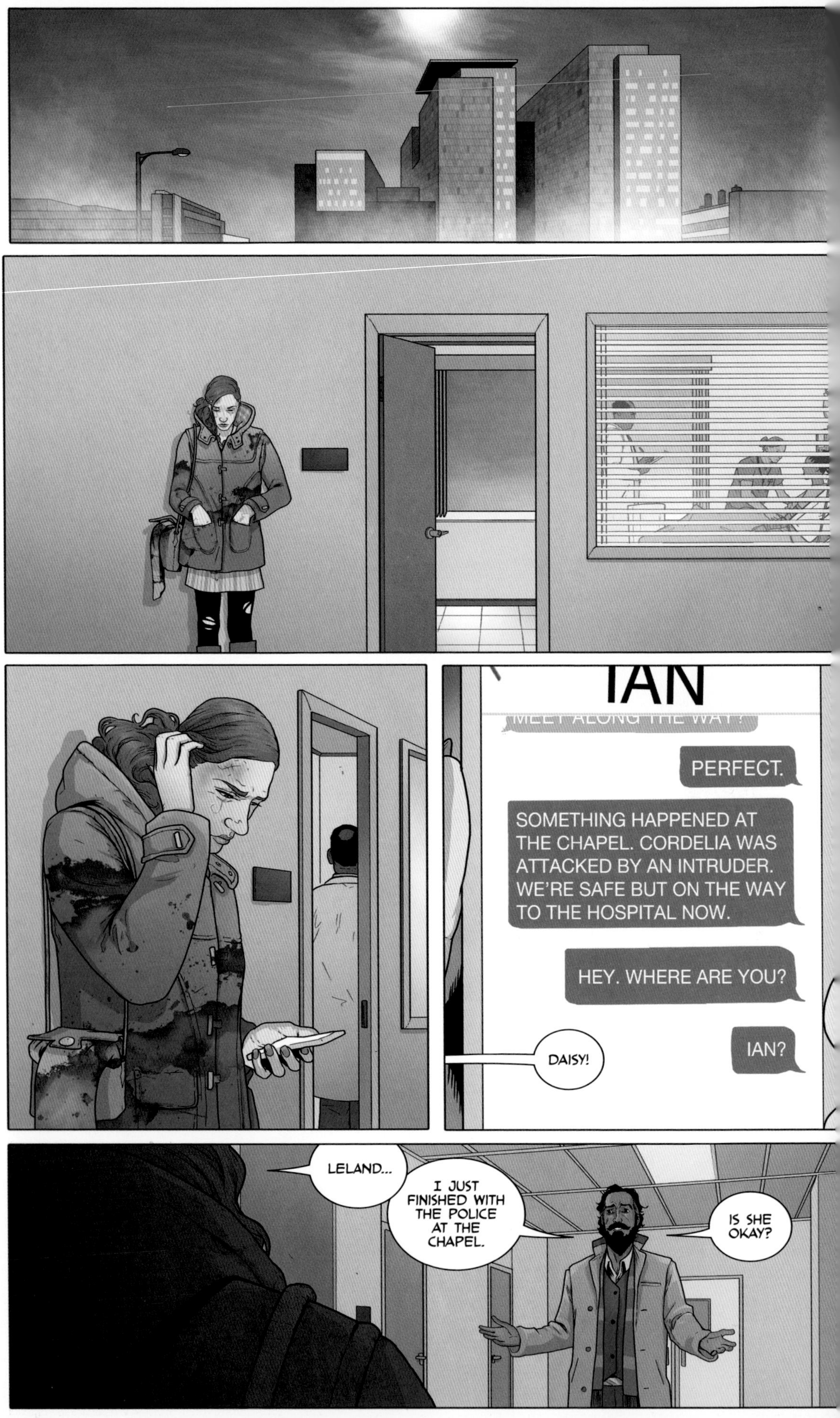
IAN
PERFECT.
SOMETHING HAPPENED AT THE CHAPEL. CORDELIA WAS ATTACKED BY AN INTRUDER. WE'RE SAFE BUT ON THE WAY TO THE HOSPITAL NOW.
HEY. WHERE ARE YOU?
IAN?
DAISY!
LELAND...
I JUST FINISHED WITH THE POLICE AT THE CHAPEL.
IS SHE OKAY?

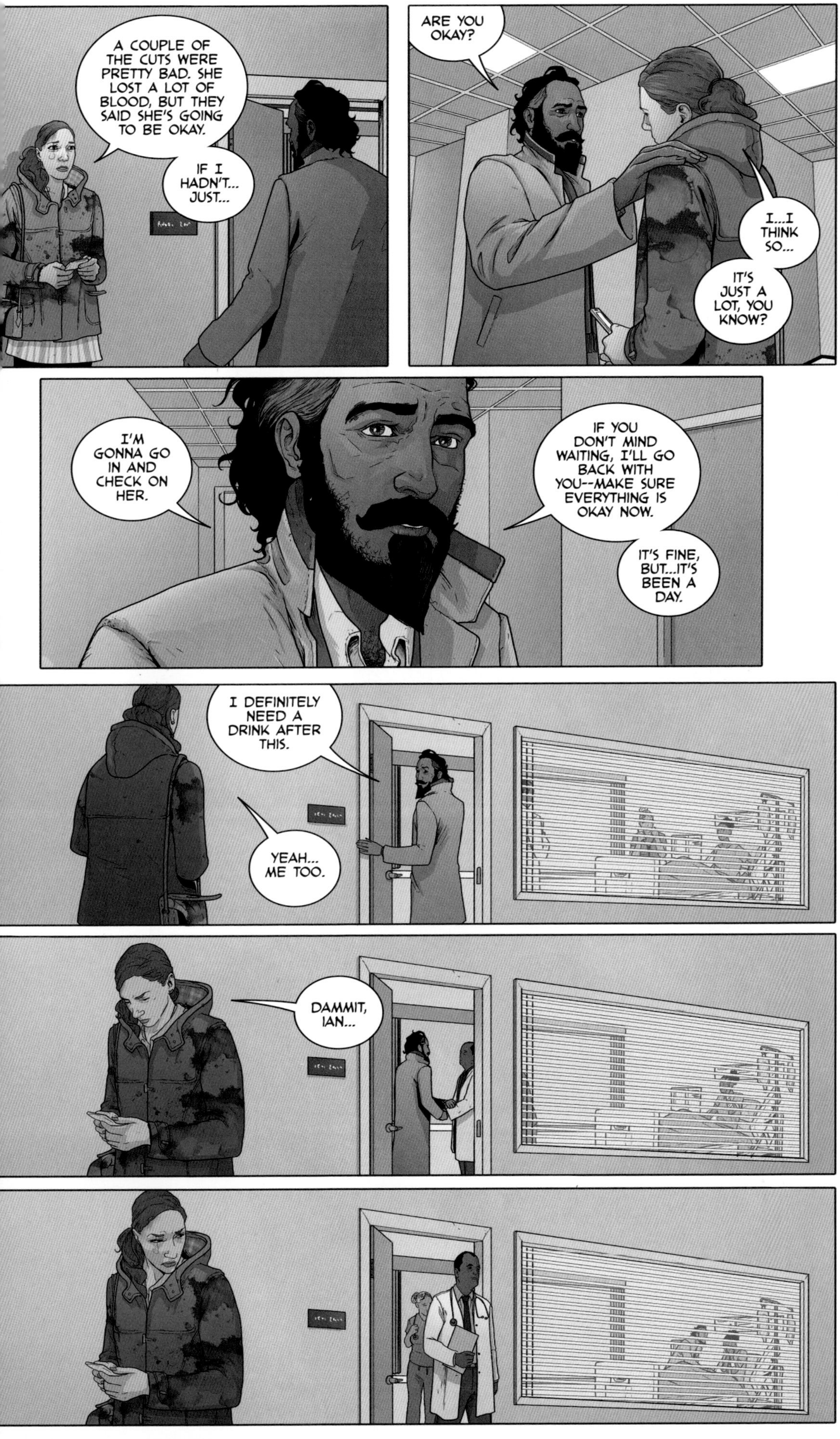
A COUPLE OF THE CUTS WERE PRETTY BAD. SHE LOST A LOT OF BLOOD, BUT THEY SAID SHE'S GOING TO BE OKAY.
IF I HADN'T... JUST...
ARE YOU OKAY?
I...I THINK SO...
IT'S JUST A LOT, YOU KNOW?
I'M GONNA GO IN AND CHECK ON HER.
IF YOU DON'T MIND WAITING, I'LL GO BACK WITH YOU--MAKE SURE EVERYTHING IS OKAY NOW.
IT'S FINE, BUT...IT'S BEEN A DAY.
I DEFINITELY NEED A DRINK AFTER THIS.
YEAH... ME TOO.
DAMMIT, IAN...

AH, HELL....

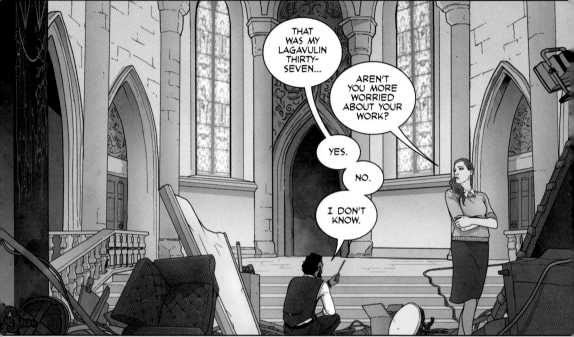

THAT WAS MY LAGAVULIN THIRTY-SEVEN...

AREN'T YOU MORE WORRIED ABOUT YOUR WORK?

YES.

NO.

I DON'T KNOW.

WE'RE A WEEK OUT FROM THE GREAT OPENING. I'VE HAD TIGHTER DEADLINES.

SURE, SOME OF THE PIECES ARE RUINED. I'LL REDO THEM. BETTER, EVEN.

ONLY THING THAT MATTERS HERE IS THAT YOU AND CORDELIA ARE OKAY.

THAT'S IT.

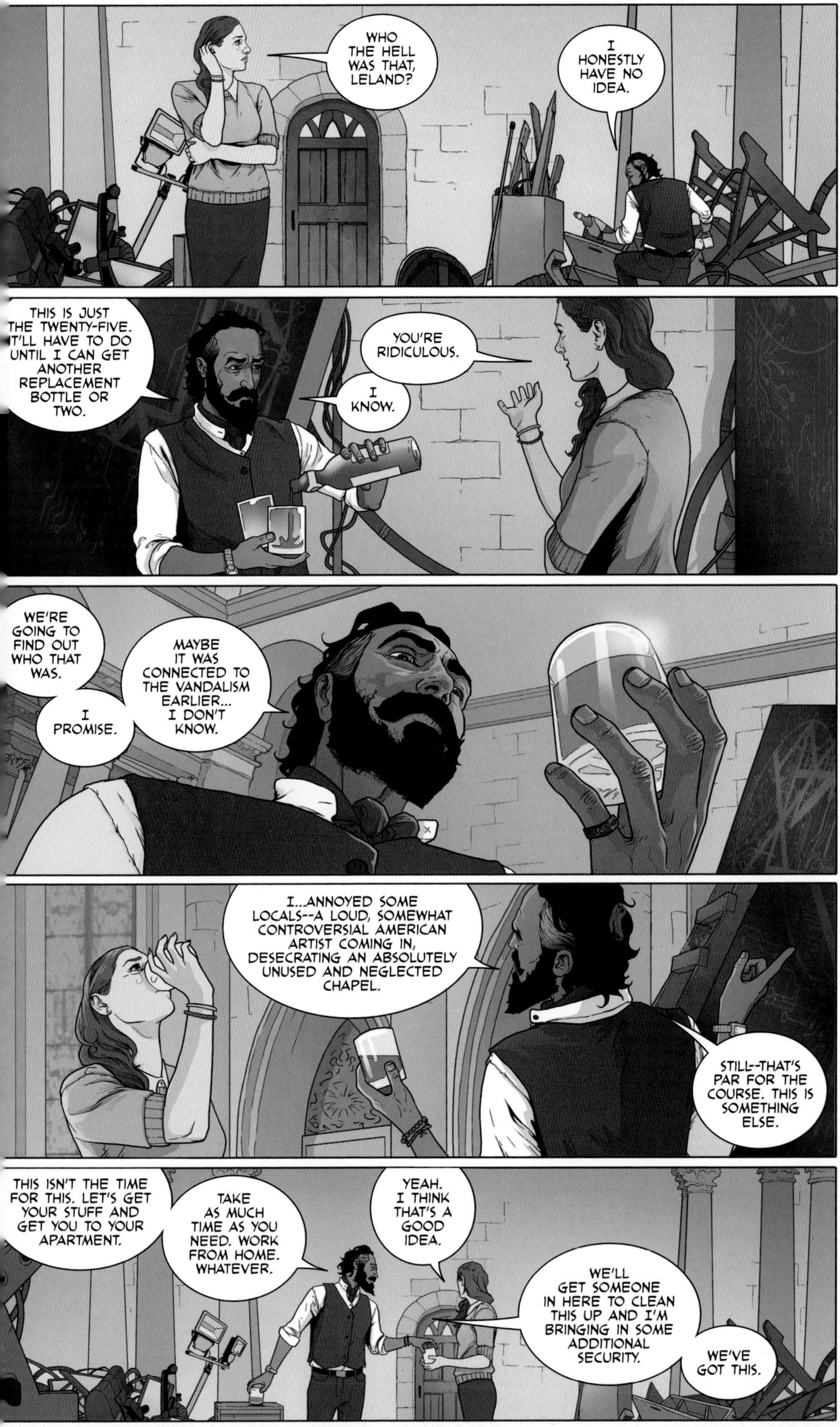
WHO THE HELL WAS THAT, LELAND?
I HONESTLY HAVE NO IDEA.
THIS IS JUST THE TWENTY-FIVE. IT'LL HAVE TO DO UNTIL I CAN GET ANOTHER REPLACEMENT BOTTLE OR TWO.
YOU'RE RIDICULOUS.
I KNOW.
WE'RE GOING TO FIND OUT WHO THAT WAS.
I PROMISE.
MAYBE IT WAS CONNECTED TO THE VANDALISM EARLIER... I DON'T KNOW.
I...ANNOYED SOME LOCALS--A LOUD, SOMEWHAT CONTROVERSIAL AMERICAN ARTIST COMING IN, DESECRATING AN ABSOLUTELY UNUSED AND NEGLECTED CHAPEL.
STILL--THAT'S PAR FOR THE COURSE. THIS IS SOMETHING ELSE.
THIS ISN'T THE TIME FOR THIS. LET'S GET YOUR STUFF AND GET YOU TO YOUR APARTMENT.
TAKE AS MUCH TIME AS YOU NEED. WORK FROM HOME. WHATEVER.
YEAH. I THINK THAT'S A GOOD IDEA.
WE'LL GET SOMEONE IN HERE TO CLEAN THIS UP AND I'M BRINGING IN SOME ADDITIONAL SECURITY.
WE'VE GOT THIS.

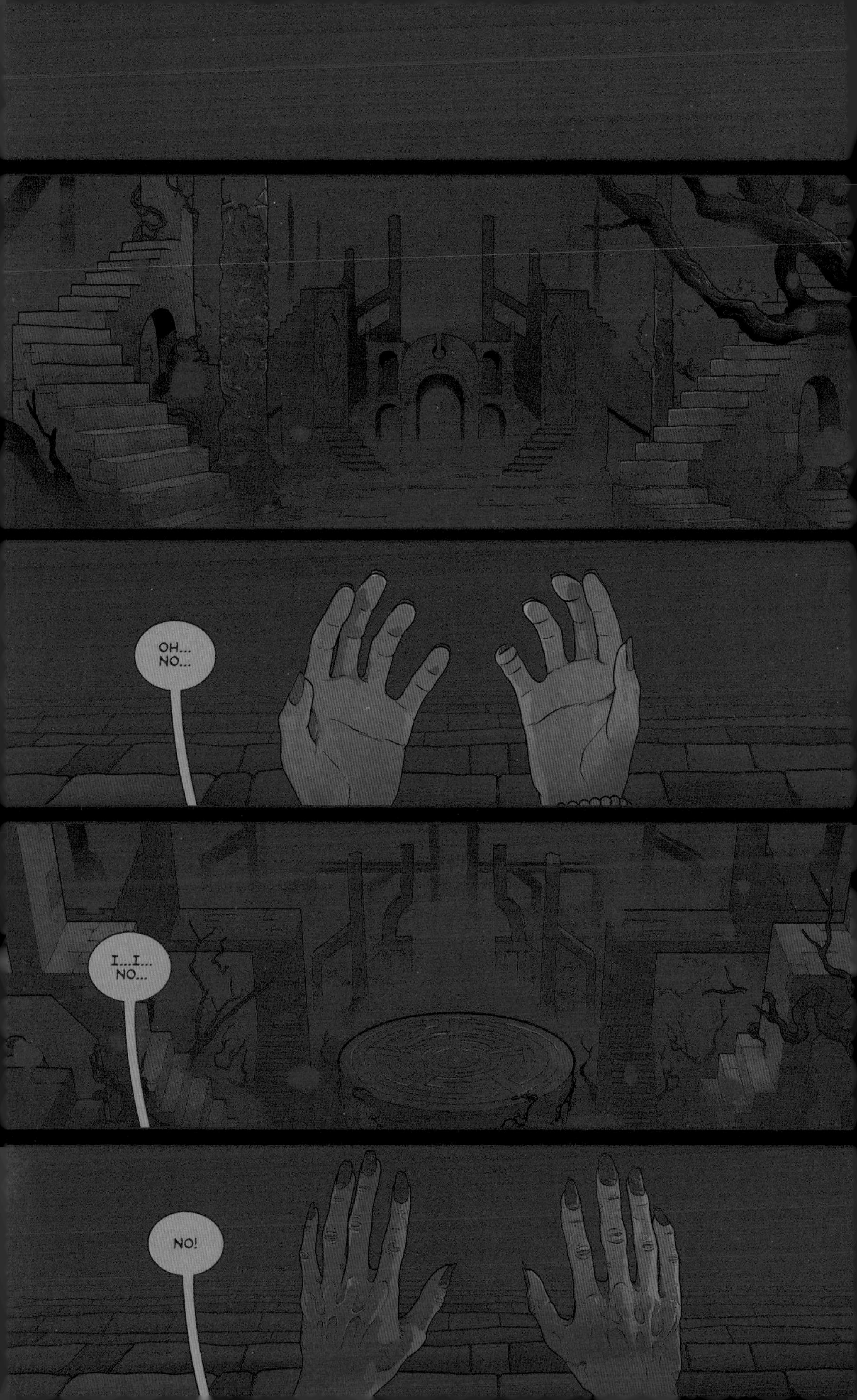
OH... NO...
I...I... NO...
NO!

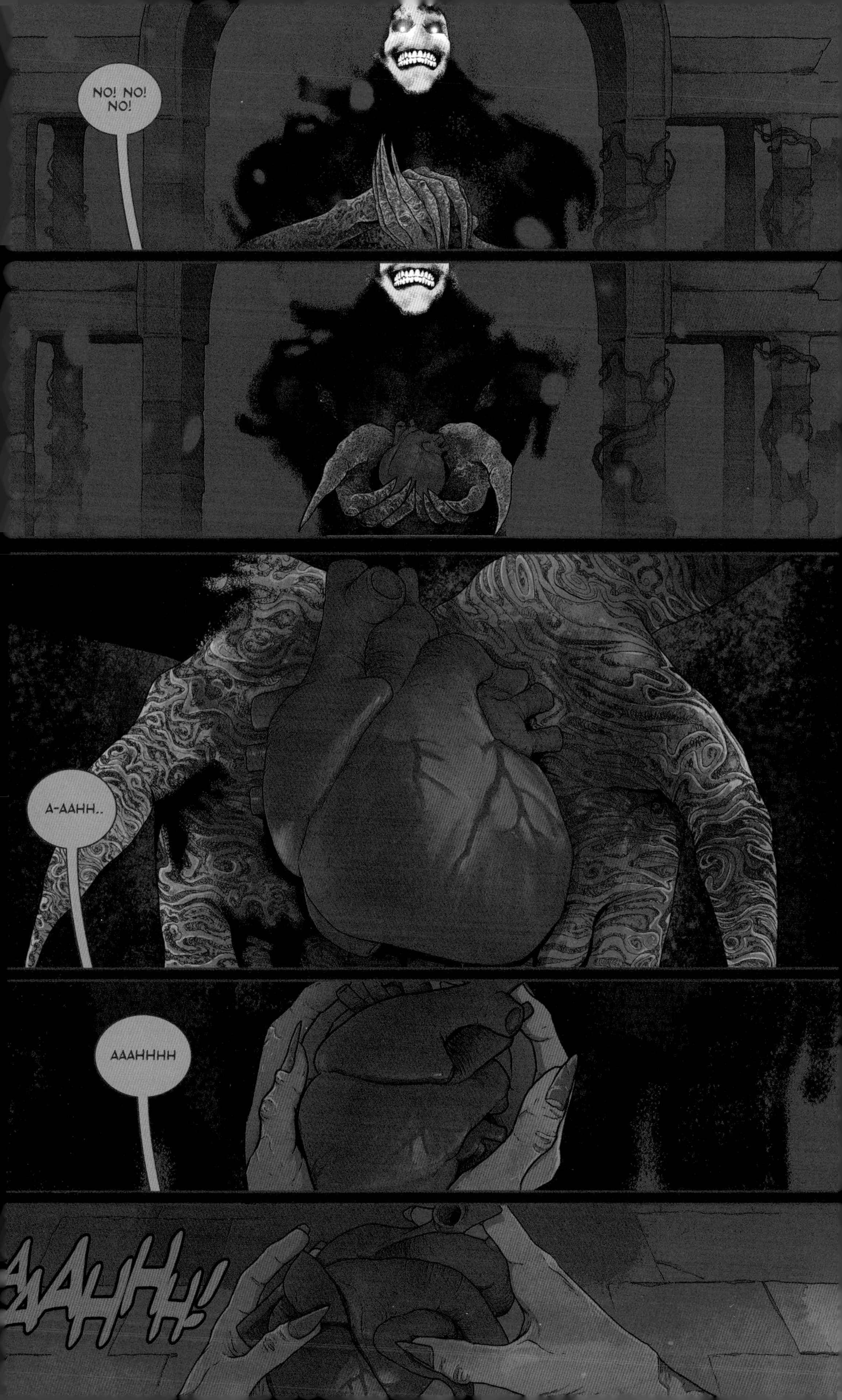
NO! NO! NO!
A-AAHH..
AAAHHHH
AAAHHH!

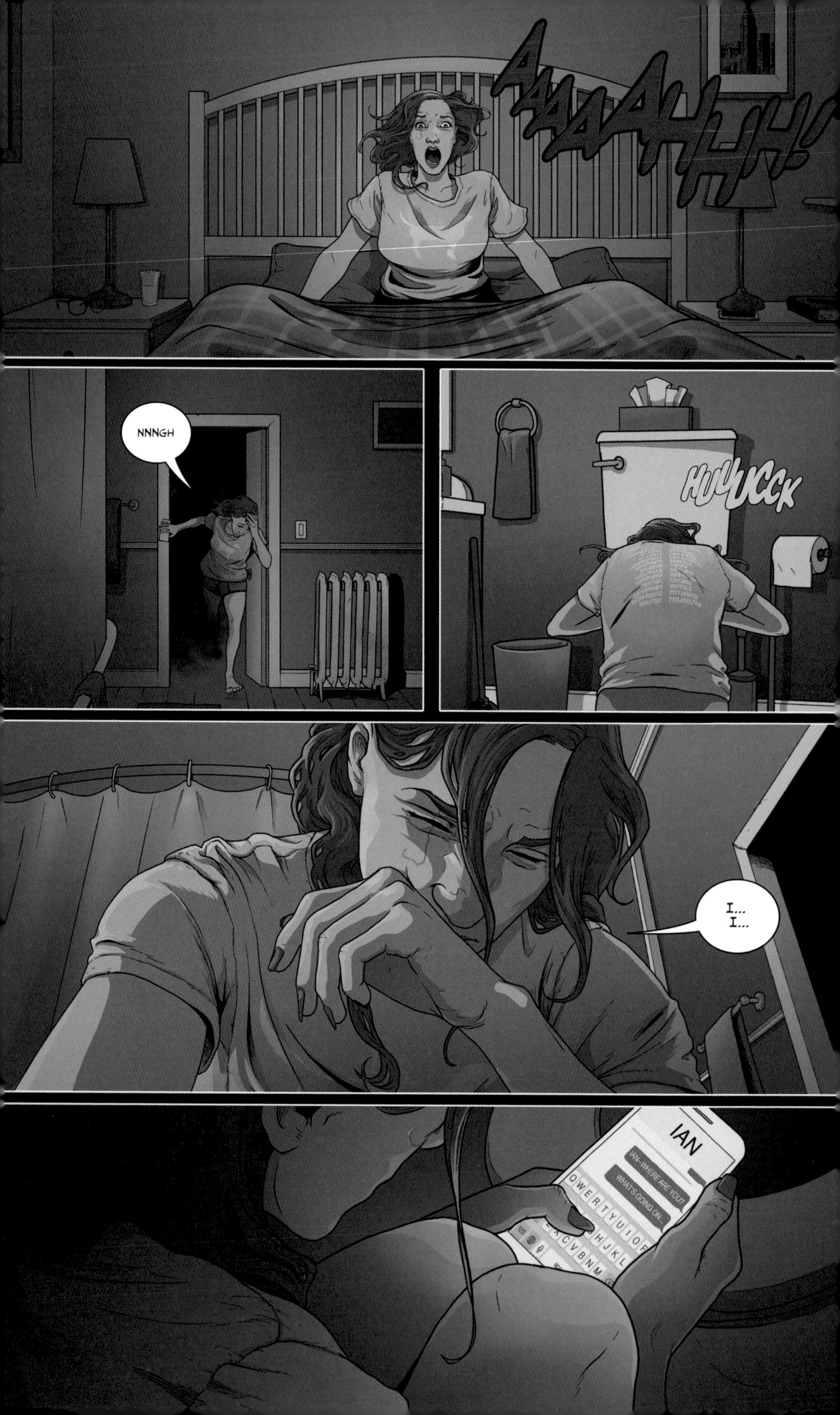
AAAAAHHH
NNNGH
HULUCCK
I... I...
IAN
IAN—WHERE ARE YOU?
WHAT'S GOING ON...

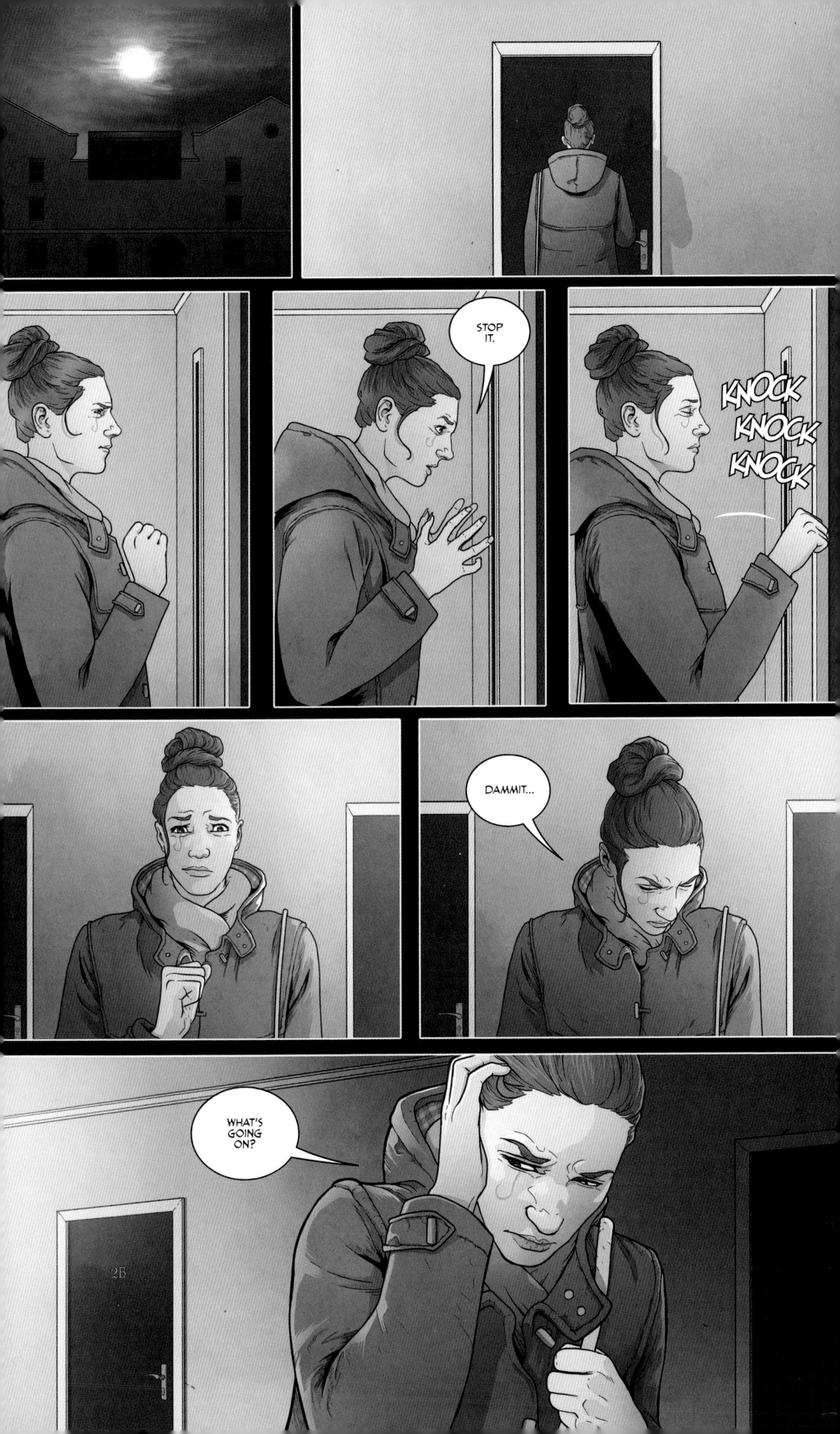
STOP IT.
KNOCK KNOCK KNOCK
DAMMIT...
WHAT'S GOING ON?
2B

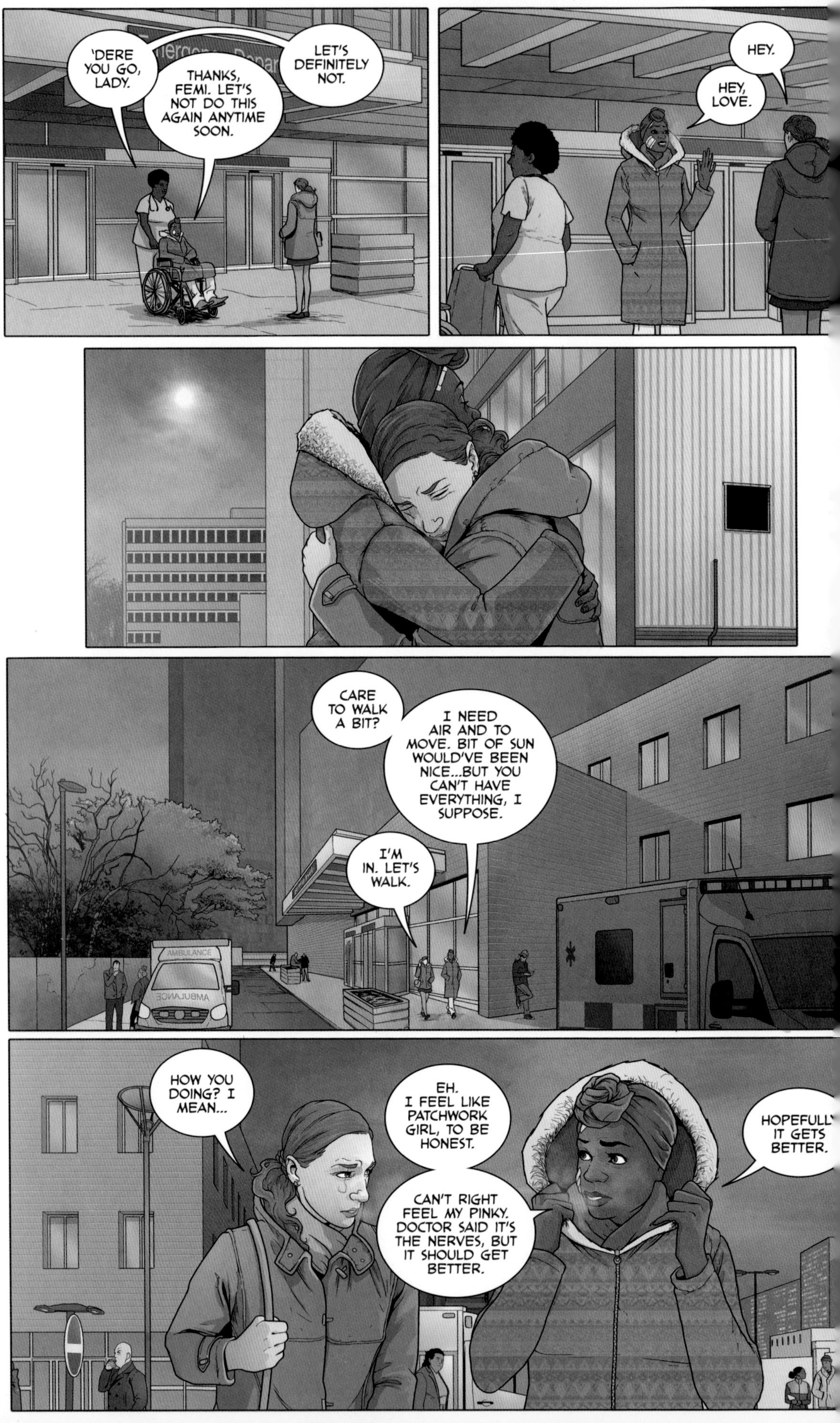

'DERE YOU GO, LADY.
THANKS, FEMI. LET'S NOT DO THIS AGAIN ANYTIME SOON.
LET'S DEFINITELY NOT.
HEY, LOVE.
HEY.
CARE TO WALK A BIT?
I NEED AIR AND TO MOVE. BIT OF SUN WOULD'VE BEEN NICE...BUT YOU CAN'T HAVE EVERYTHING, I SUPPOSE.
I'M IN. LET'S WALK.
HOW YOU DOING? I MEAN...
EH. I FEEL LIKE PATCHWORK GIRL, TO BE HONEST.
CAN'T RIGHT FEEL MY PINKY. DOCTOR SAID IT'S THE NERVES, BUT IT SHOULD GET BETTER.
HOPEFULL IT GETS BETTER.

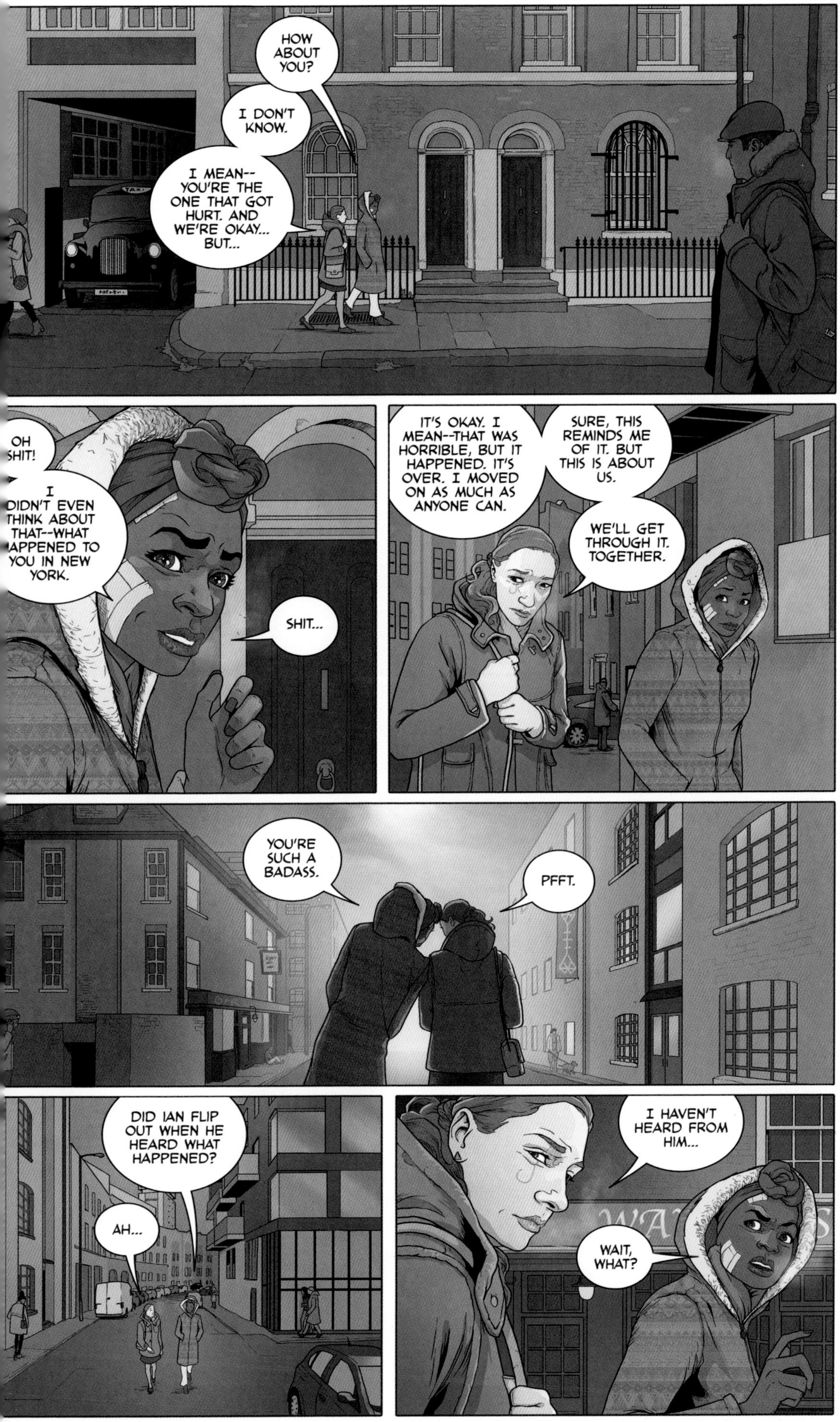
HOW ABOUT YOU?
I DON'T KNOW.
I MEAN-- YOU'RE THE ONE THAT GOT HURT. AND WE'RE OKAY... BUT...
OH SHIT!
I DIDN'T EVEN THINK ABOUT THAT--WHAT HAPPENED TO YOU IN NEW YORK.
SHIT...
IT'S OKAY. I MEAN--THAT WAS HORRIBLE, BUT IT HAPPENED. IT'S OVER. I MOVED ON AS MUCH AS ANYONE CAN.
SURE, THIS REMINDS ME OF IT. BUT THIS IS ABOUT US.
WE'LL GET THROUGH IT. TOGETHER.
YOU'RE SUCH A BADASS.
PFFT.
DID IAN FLIP OUT WHEN HE HEARD WHAT HAPPENED?
AH...
I HAVEN'T HEARD FROM HIM...
WAIT, WHAT?

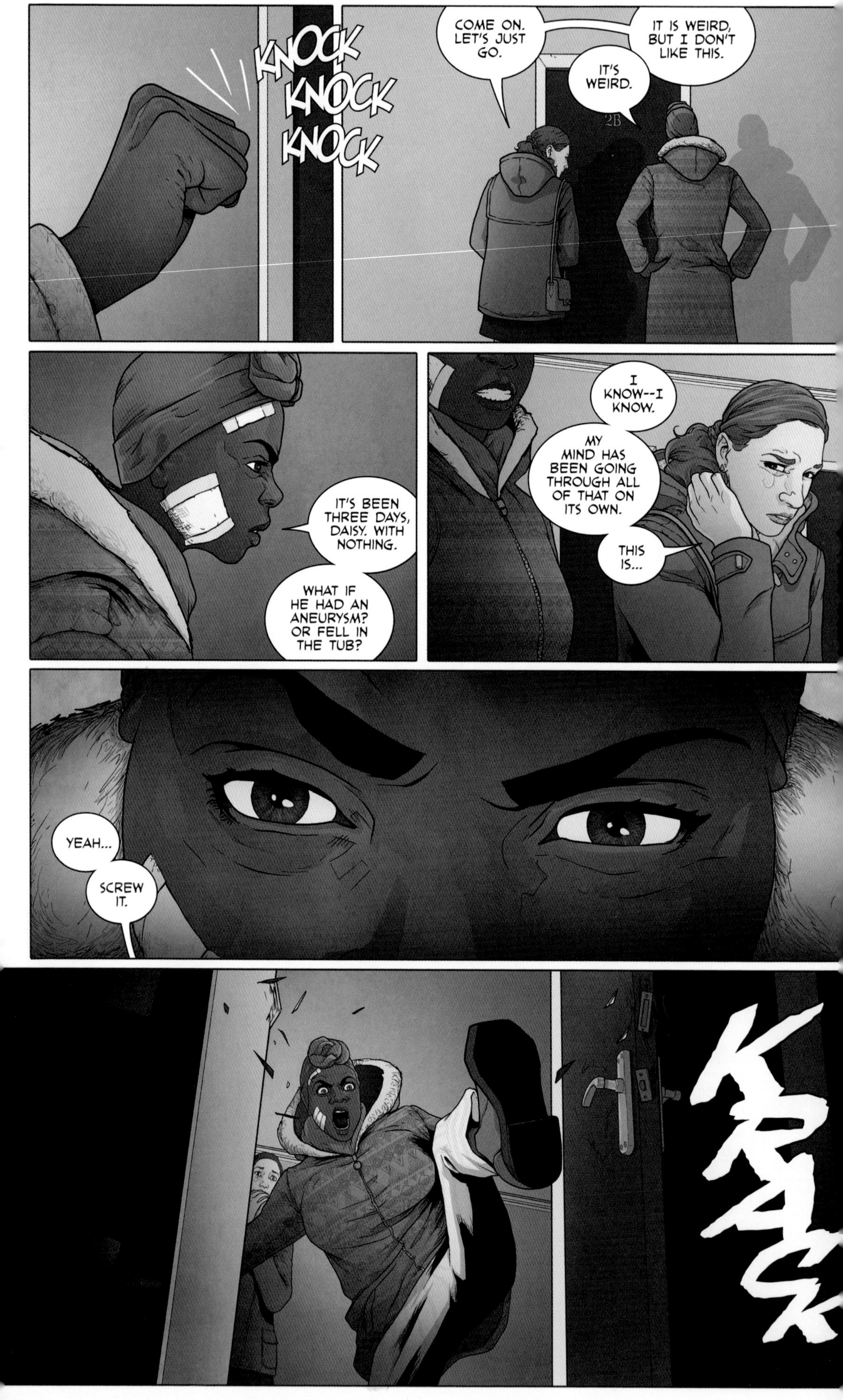
KNOCK KNOCK KNOCK
COME ON. LET'S JUST GO.
IT IS WEIRD, BUT I DON'T LIKE THIS.
IT'S WEIRD.
2B
IT'S BEEN THREE DAYS, DAISY. WITH NOTHING.
WHAT IF HE HAD AN ANEURYSM? OR FELL IN THE TUB?
I KNOW--I KNOW.
MY MIND HAS BEEN GOING THROUGH ALL OF THAT ON ITS OWN.
THIS IS...
YEAH...
SCREW IT.
KRACK

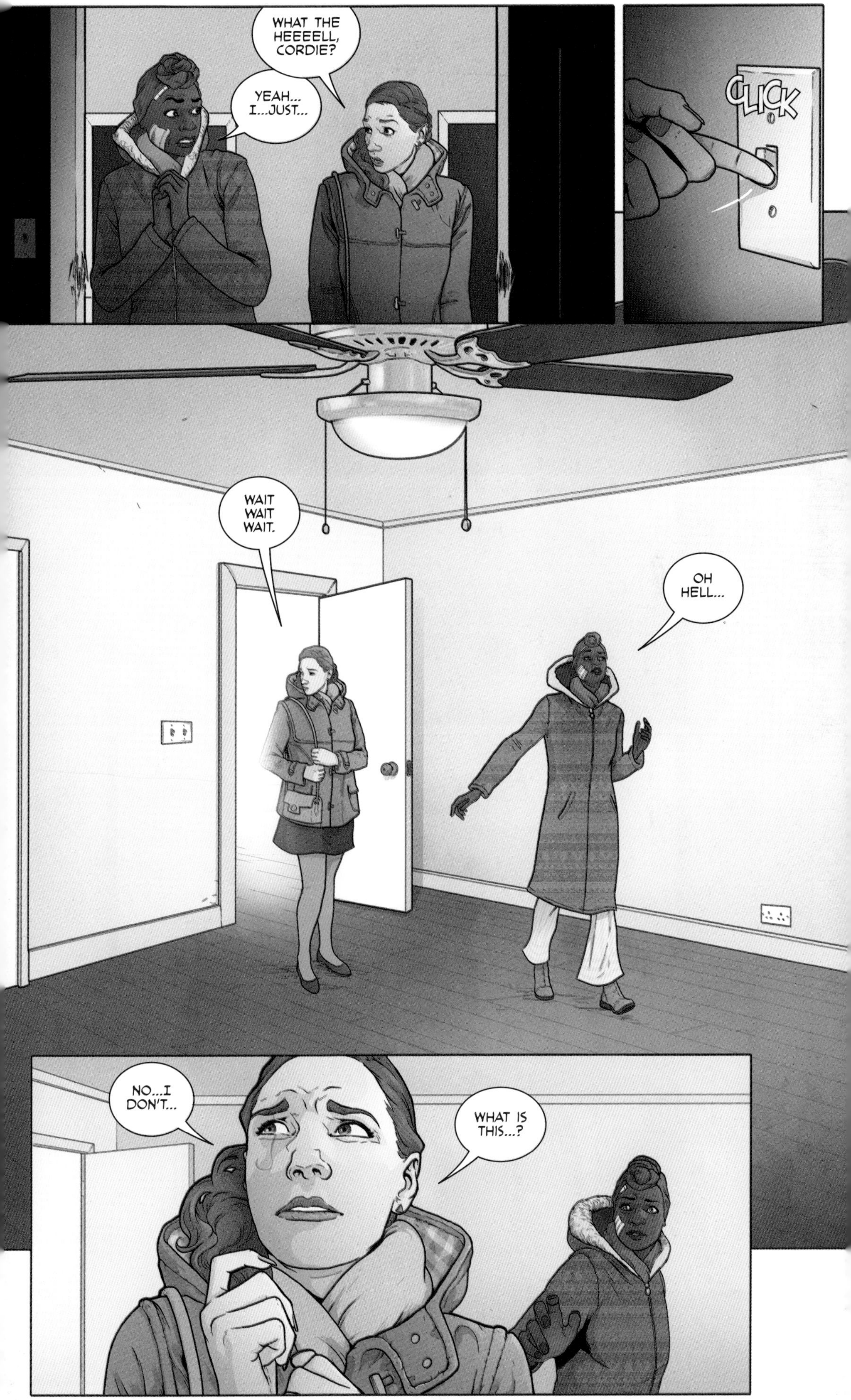
WHAT THE HEEEELL, CORDIE?
YEAH... I...JUST...
CLICK
WAIT WAIT WAIT.
OH HELL...
NO...I DON'T...
WHAT IS THIS...?

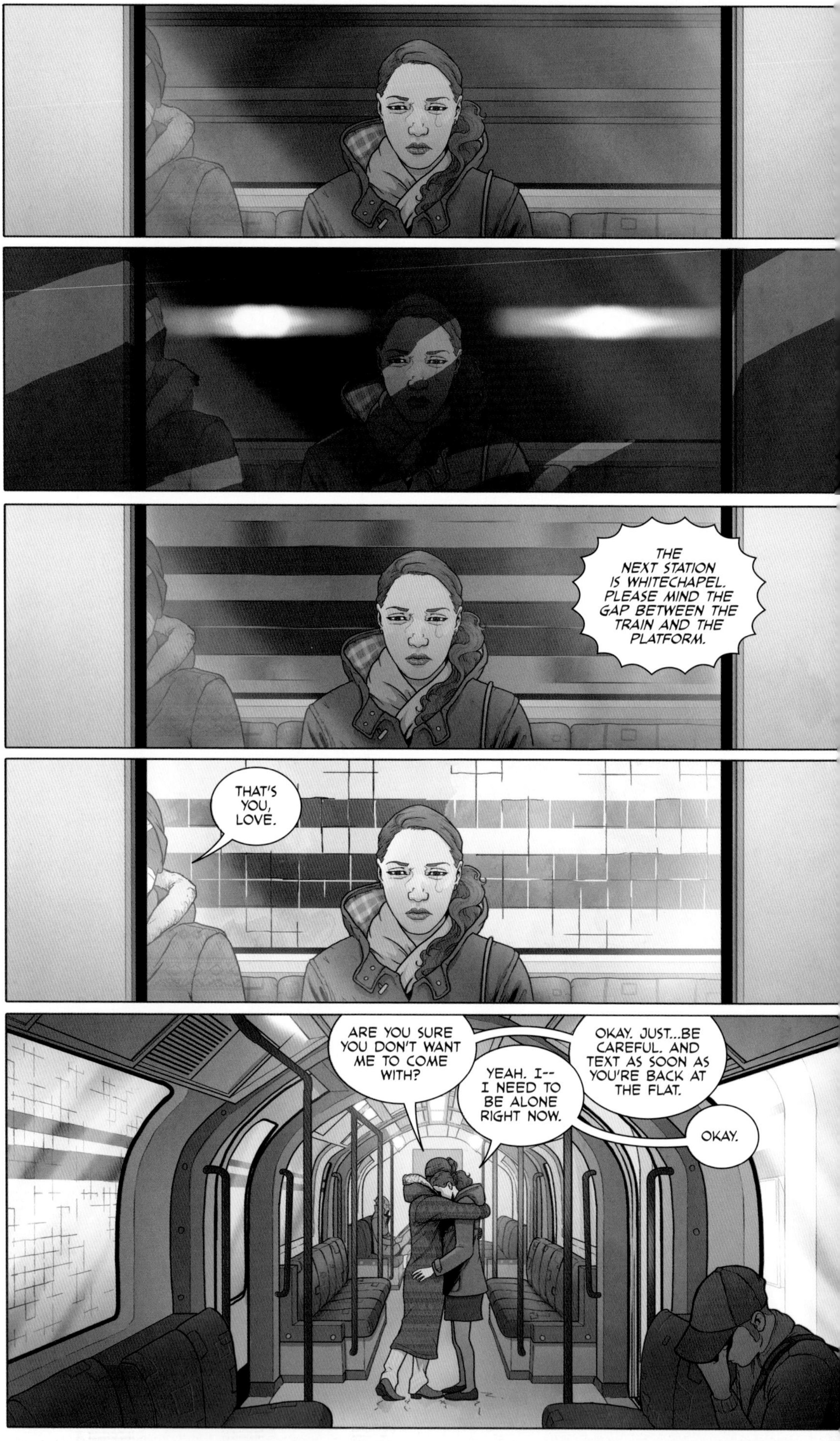
THE NEXT STATION IS WHITECHAPEL. PLEASE MIND THE GAP BETWEEN THE TRAIN AND THE PLATFORM.
THAT'S YOU, LOVE.
ARE YOU SURE YOU DON'T WANT ME TO COME WITH?
YEAH. I-- I NEED TO BE ALONE RIGHT NOW.
OKAY. JUST...BE CAREFUL. AND TEXT AS SOON AS YOU'RE BACK AT THE FLAT.
OKAY.

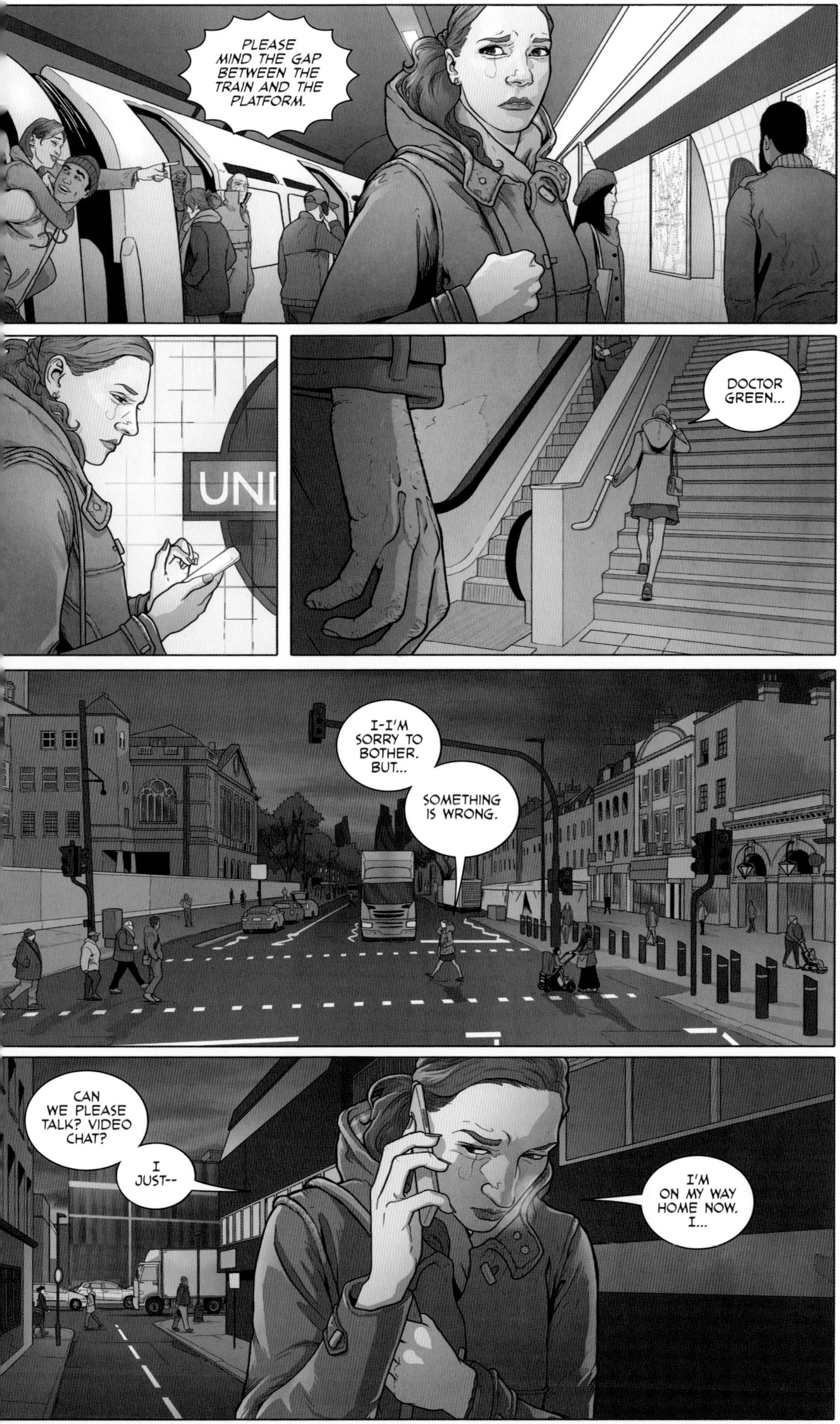
PLEASE MIND THE GAP BETWEEN THE TRAIN AND THE PLATFORM.
UND
DOCTOR GREEN...
I-I'M SORRY TO BOTHER. BUT...
SOMETHING IS WRONG.
CAN WE PLEASE TALK? VIDEO CHAT?
I JUST--
I'M ON MY WAY HOME NOW. I...

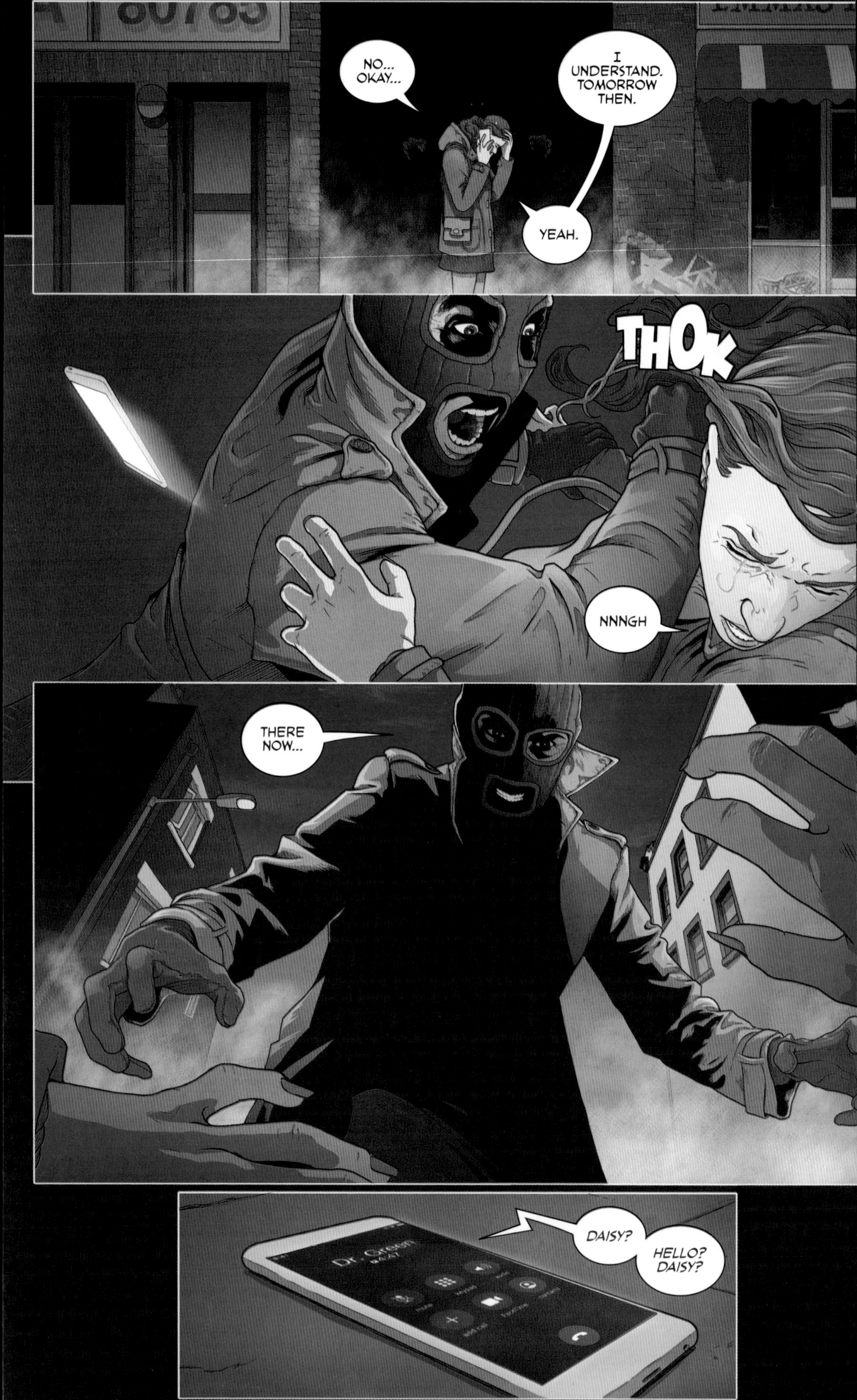
NO... OKAY...
I UNDERSTAND. TOMORROW THEN.
YEAH.
THOK
NNNGH
THERE NOW...
DAISY?
HELLO? DAISY?

CHAPTER
TEN

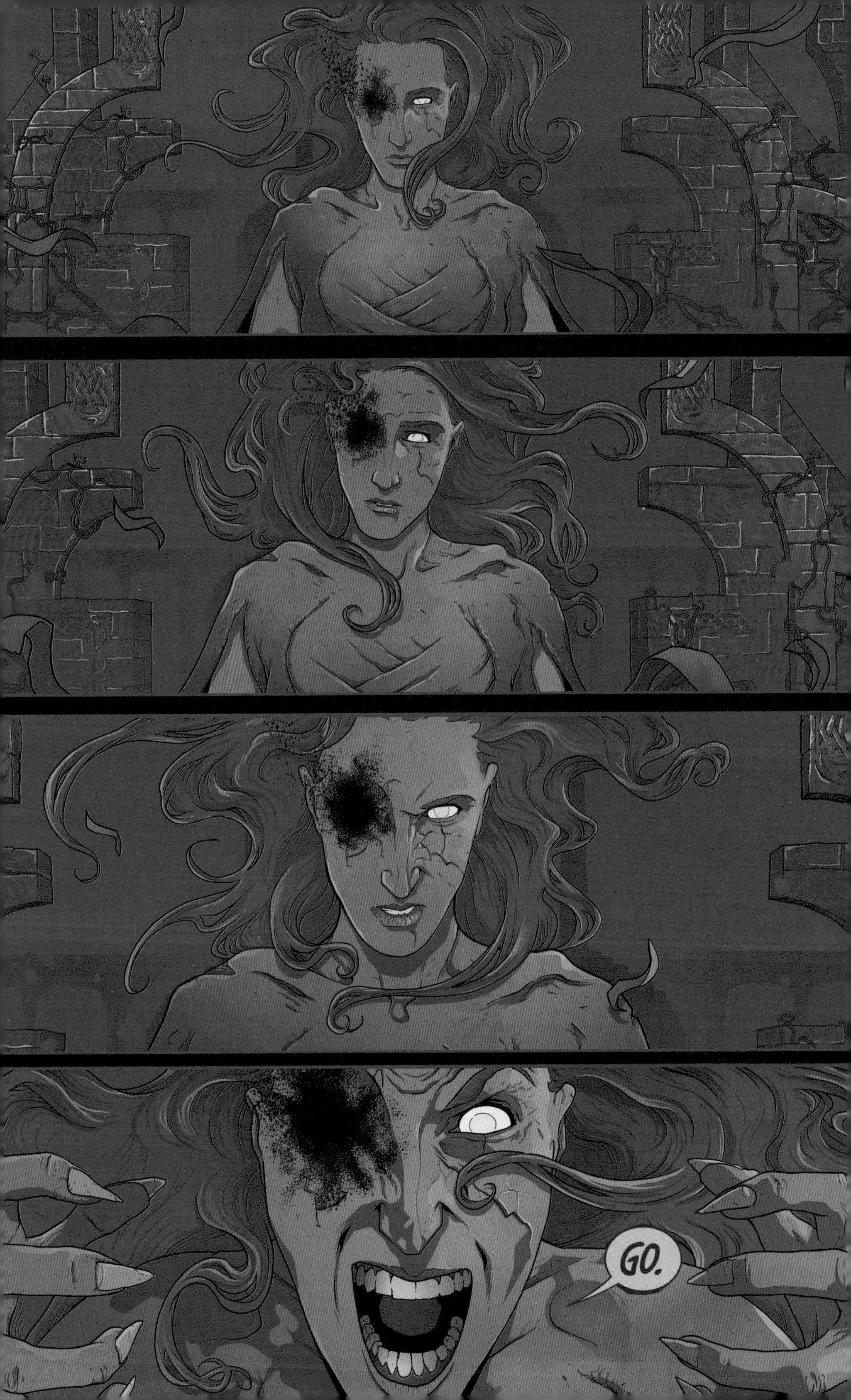
GO.

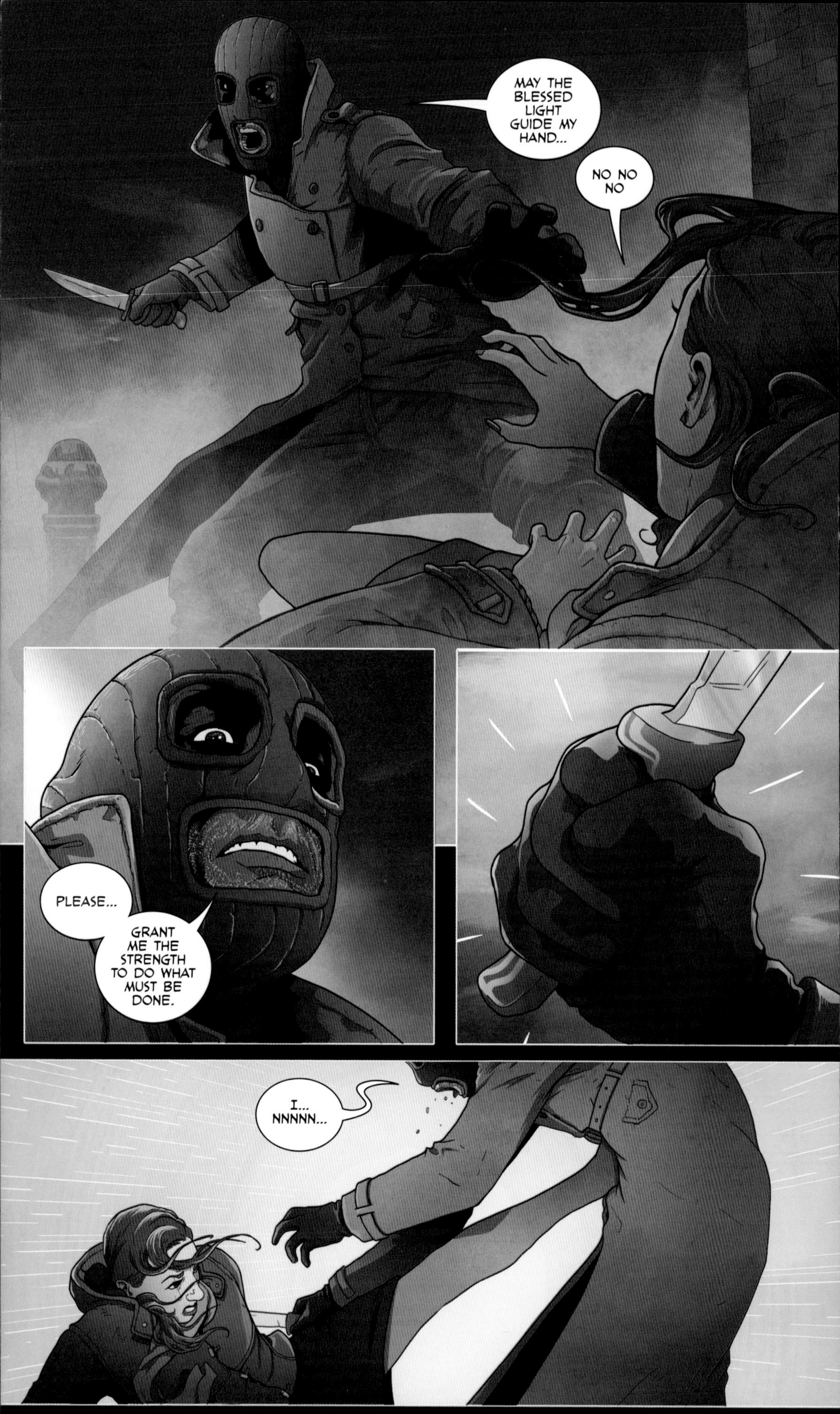
MAY THE BLESSED LIGHT GUIDE MY HAND...
NO NO NO
PLEASE...
GRANT ME THE STRENGTH TO DO WHAT MUST BE DONE.
I... NNNNN...

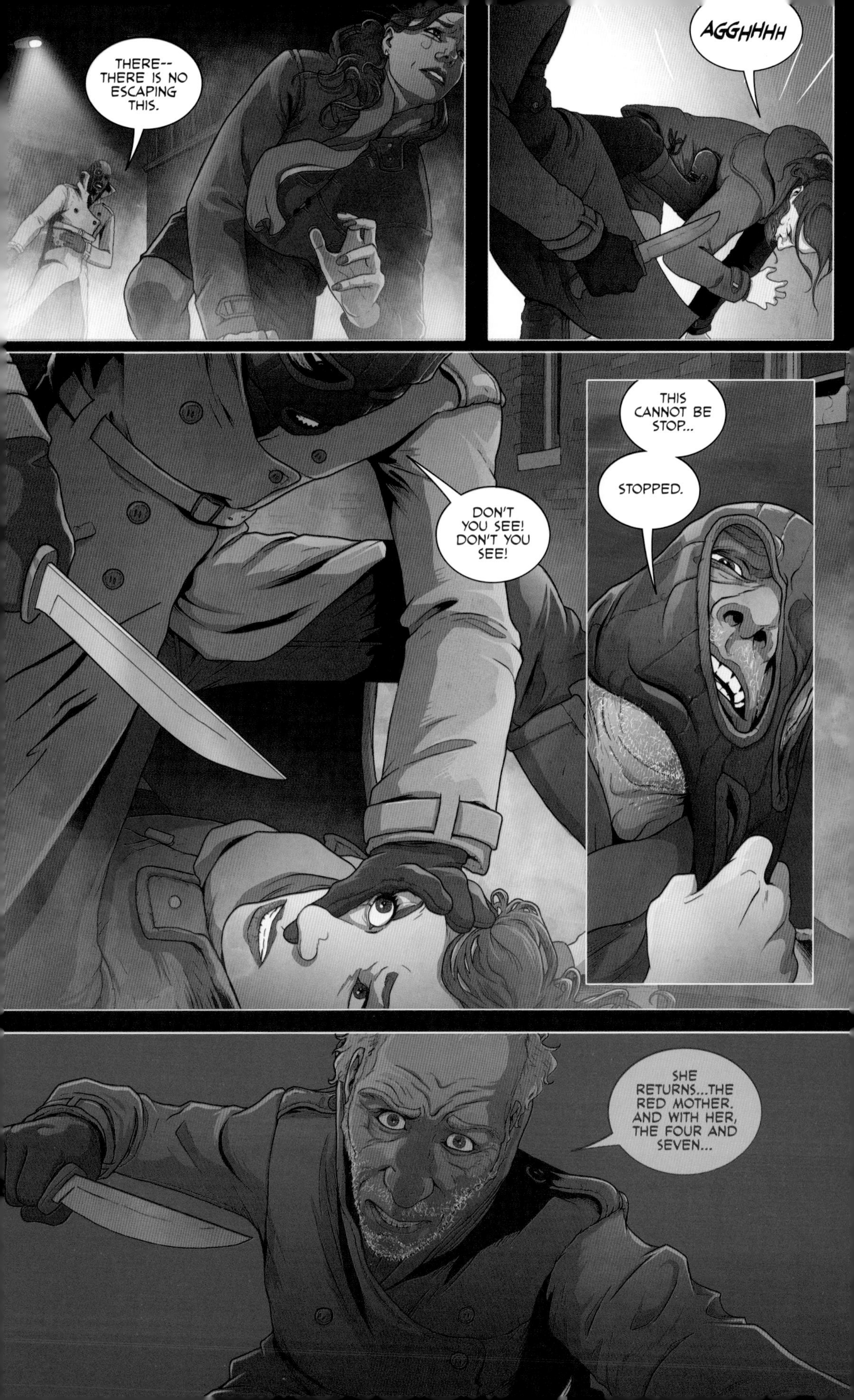
THERE-- THERE IS NO ESCAPING THIS.
AGGHHHH
DON'T YOU SEE! DON'T YOU SEE!
THIS CANNOT BE STOP...
STOPPED.
SHE RETURNS...THE RED MOTHER. AND WITH HER, THE FOUR AND SEVEN...

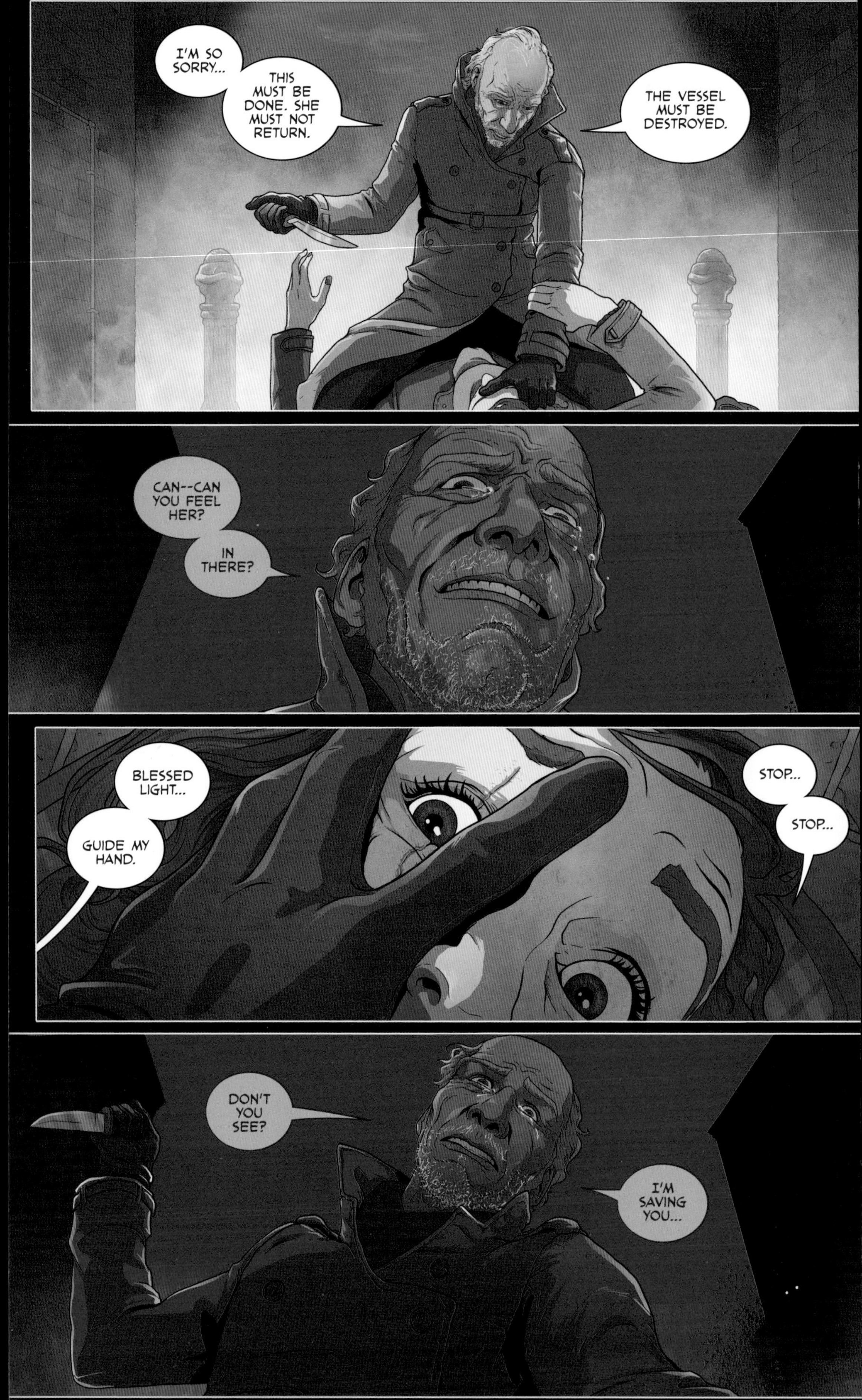
I'M SO SORRY...
THIS MUST BE DONE. SHE MUST NOT RETURN.
THE VESSEL MUST BE DESTROYED.
CAN--CAN YOU FEEL HER?
IN THERE?
BLESSED LIGHT...
GUIDE MY HAND.
STOP...
STOP...
DON'T YOU SEE?
I'M SAVING YOU...

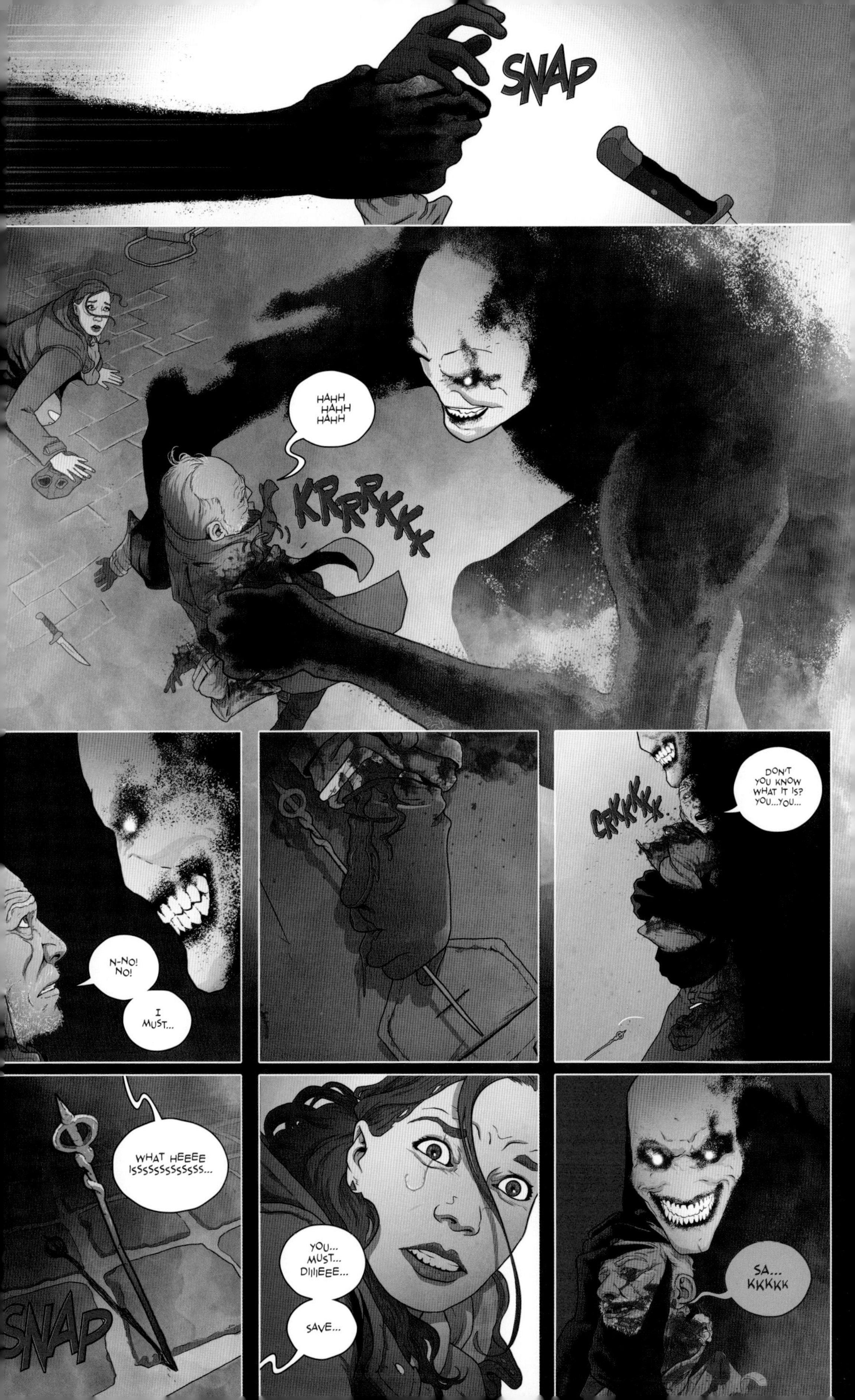
SNAP
HAHH HAHH HAHH
KRRRKKK
N-NO! NO!
I MUST...
CRKKKK
DON'T YOU KNOW WHAT IT IS? YOU...YOU...
WHAT HEEEE ISSSSSSSSSSS...
SNAP
YOU... MUST... DIIIIEEE...
SAVE...
SA... KKKKK

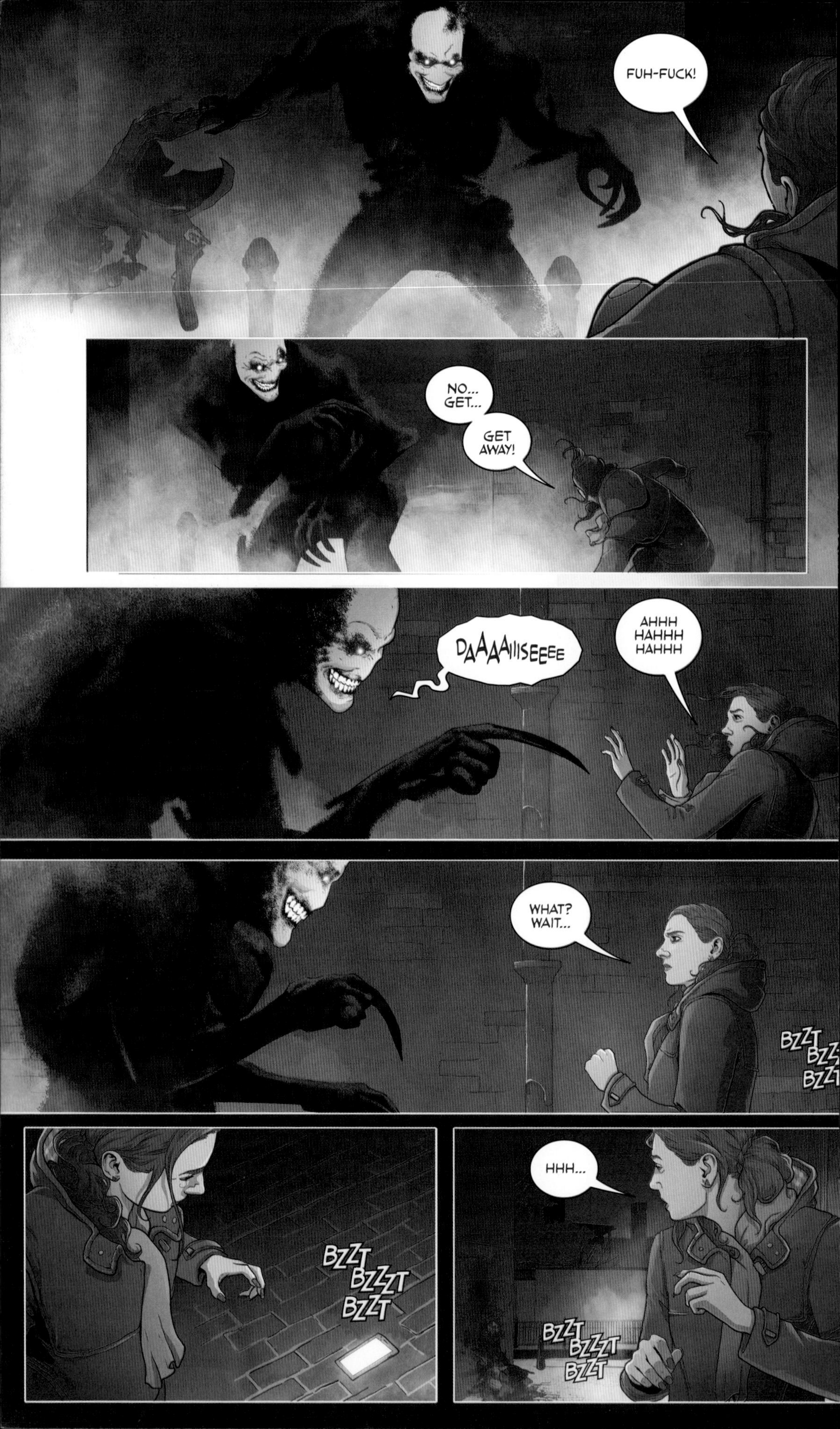
FUH-FUCK!
NO... GET...
GET AWAY!
DAAAAIIISEEEE
AHHH HAHHH HAHHH
WHAT? WAIT...
BZZT BZZ- BZZT
BZZT BZZZT BZZT
HHH...
BZZT BZZZT BZZT

WHAT THE HELL...
THIS...
THIS...
BZZT BZZZT BZZT
Dr. Green
BZZT BZZZT BZZT
BZZT BZZZ...

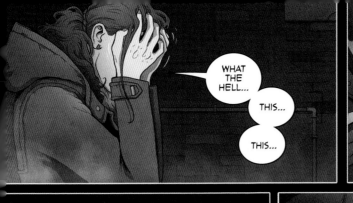

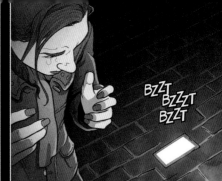

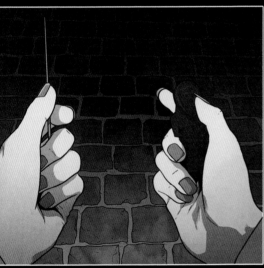

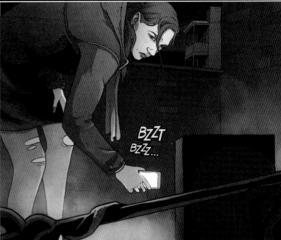

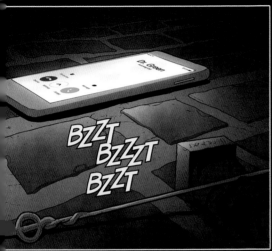

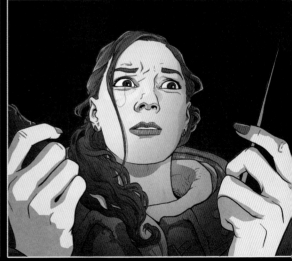

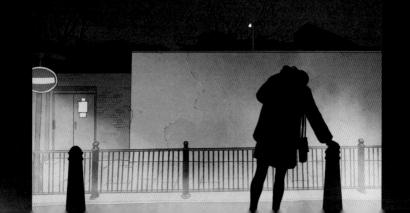

BZZT

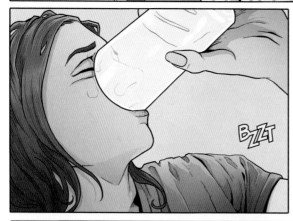

BZZT

SEVENTY FOUR TEXTS...

JEEZE.

THURSDAY?!

YOU SLEPT MORE THAN AN ENTIRE DAY...

DAMMIT.

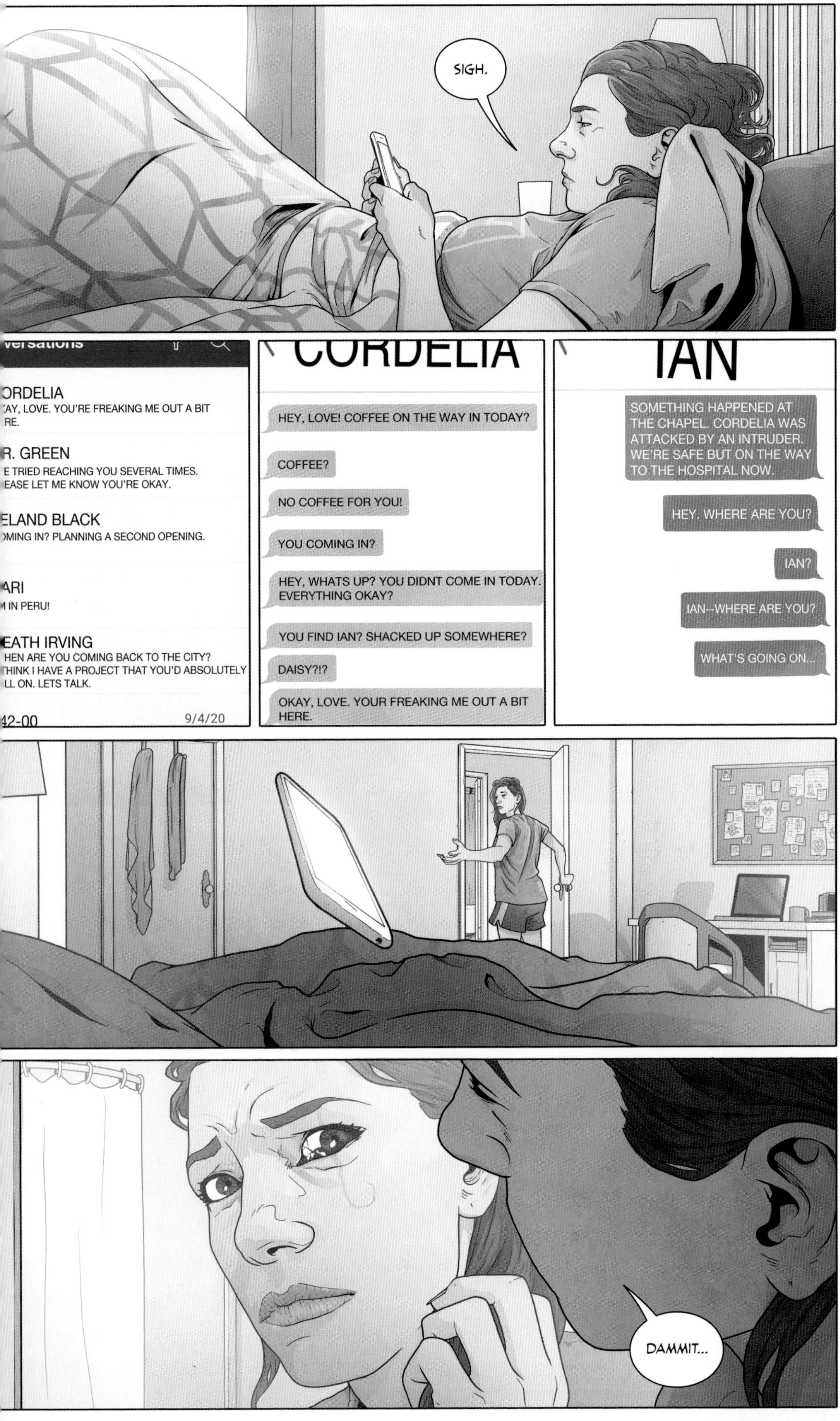
SIGH.
ORDELIA
AY, LOVE. YOU'RE FREAKING ME OUT A BIT
RE.
R. GREEN
E TRIED REACHING YOU SEVERAL TIMES.
EASE LET ME KNOW YOU'RE OKAY.
ELAND BLACK
OMING IN? PLANNING A SECOND OPENING.
ARI
I IN PERU!
EATH IRVING
HEN ARE YOU COMING BACK TO THE CITY?
THINK I HAVE A PROJECT THAT YOU'D ABSOLUTELY
LL ON. LETS TALK.
42-00
9/4/20
CORDELIA
HEY, LOVE! COFFEE ON THE WAY IN TODAY?
COFFEE?
NO COFFEE FOR YOU!
YOU COMING IN?
HEY, WHATS UP? YOU DIDNT COME IN TODAY. EVERYTHING OKAY?
YOU FIND IAN? SHACKED UP SOMEWHERE?
DAISY?!?
OKAY, LOVE. YOUR FREAKING ME OUT A BIT HERE.
IAN
SOMETHING HAPPENED AT THE CHAPEL. CORDELIA WAS ATTACKED BY AN INTRUDER. WE'RE SAFE BUT ON THE WAY TO THE HOSPITAL NOW.
HEY. WHERE ARE YOU?
IAN?
IAN--WHERE ARE YOU?
WHAT'S GOING ON...
DAMMIT...

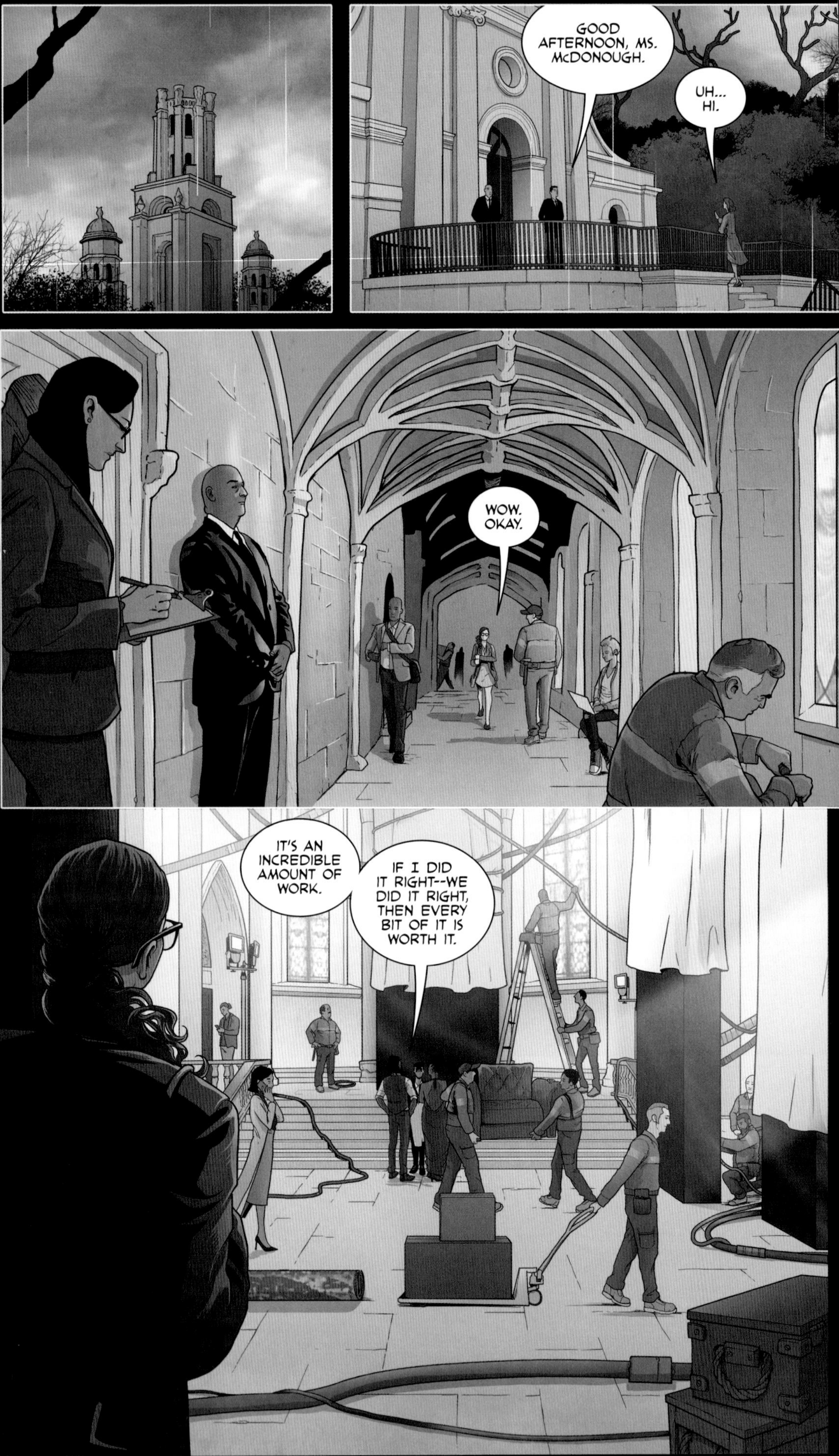
GOOD AFTERNOON, MS. McDONOUGH.
UH... HI.
WOW. OKAY.
IT'S AN INCREDIBLE AMOUNT OF WORK.
IF I DID IT RIGHT--WE DID IT RIGHT, THEN EVERY BIT OF IT IS WORTH IT.

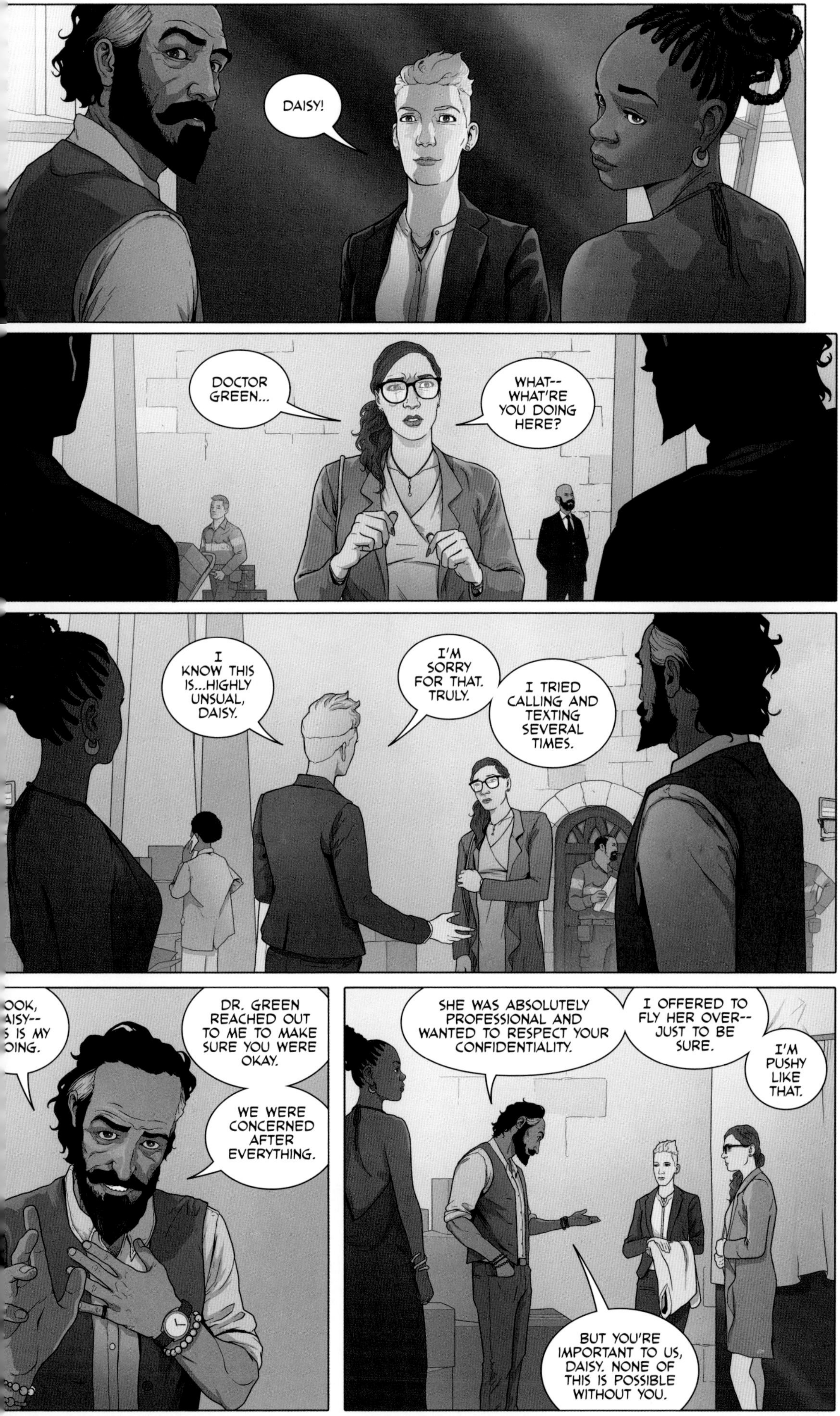
DAISY!
DOCTOR GREEN...
WHAT--
WHAT'RE YOU DOING HERE?
I KNOW THIS IS...HIGHLY UNUSUAL, DAISY.
I'M SORRY FOR THAT. TRULY.
I TRIED CALLING AND TEXTING SEVERAL TIMES.
OOK, AISY-- S IS MY OING.
DR. GREEN REACHED OUT TO ME TO MAKE SURE YOU WERE OKAY.
WE WERE CONCERNED AFTER EVERYTHING.
SHE WAS ABSOLUTELY PROFESSIONAL AND WANTED TO RESPECT YOUR CONFIDENTIALITY.
I OFFERED TO FLY HER OVER-- JUST TO BE SURE.
I'M PUSHY LIKE THAT.
BUT YOU'RE IMPORTANT TO US, DAISY. NONE OF THIS IS POSSIBLE WITHOUT YOU.

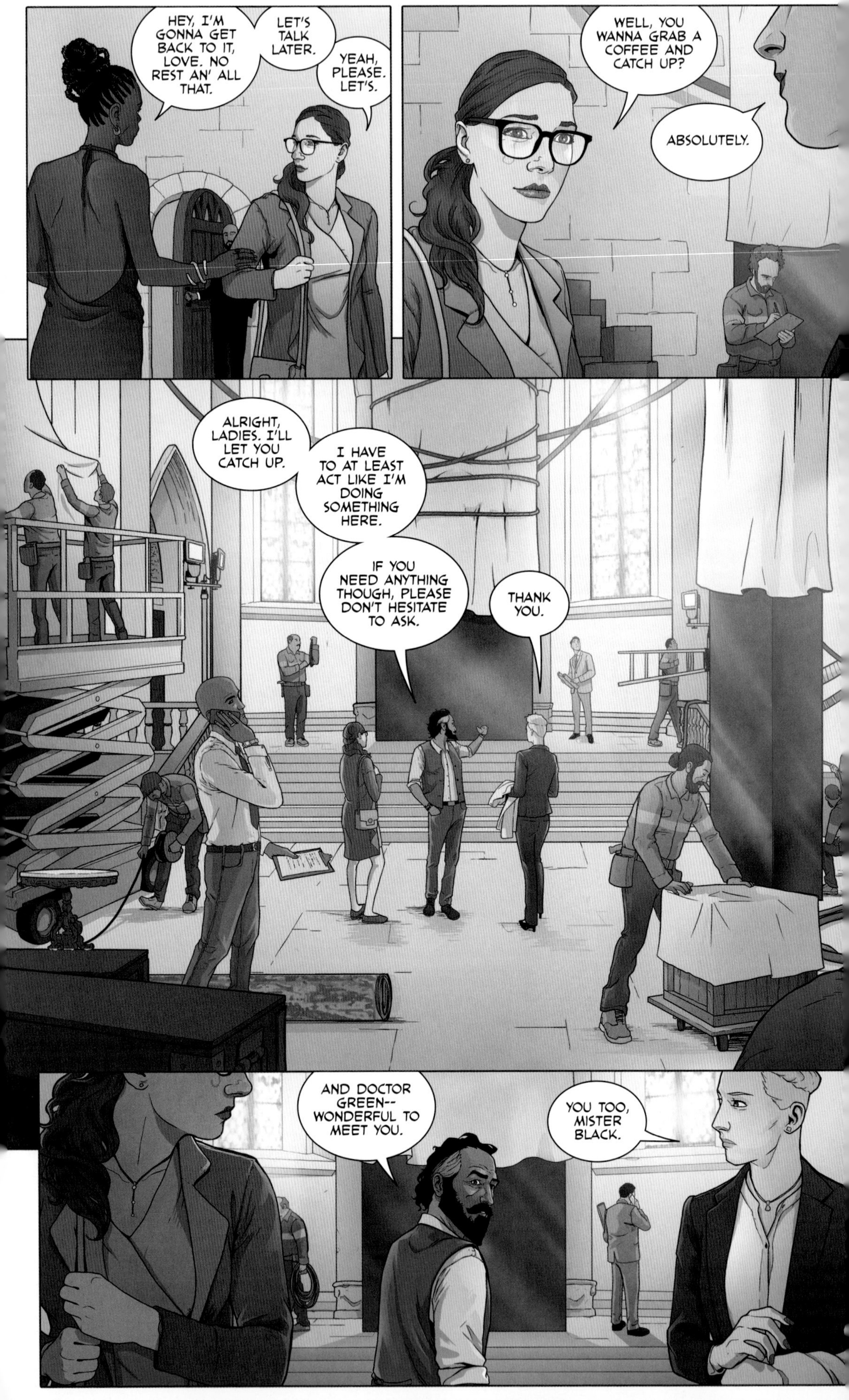
HEY, I'M GONNA GET BACK TO IT, LOVE. NO REST AN' ALL THAT.
LET'S TALK LATER.
YEAH, PLEASE. LET'S.
WELL, YOU WANNA GRAB A COFFEE AND CATCH UP?
ABSOLUTELY.
ALRIGHT, LADIES. I'LL LET YOU CATCH UP.
I HAVE TO AT LEAST ACT LIKE I'M DOING SOMETHING HERE.
IF YOU NEED ANYTHING THOUGH, PLEASE DON'T HESITATE TO ASK.
THANK YOU.
AND DOCTOR GREEN-- WONDERFUL TO MEET YOU.
YOU TOO, MISTER BLACK.

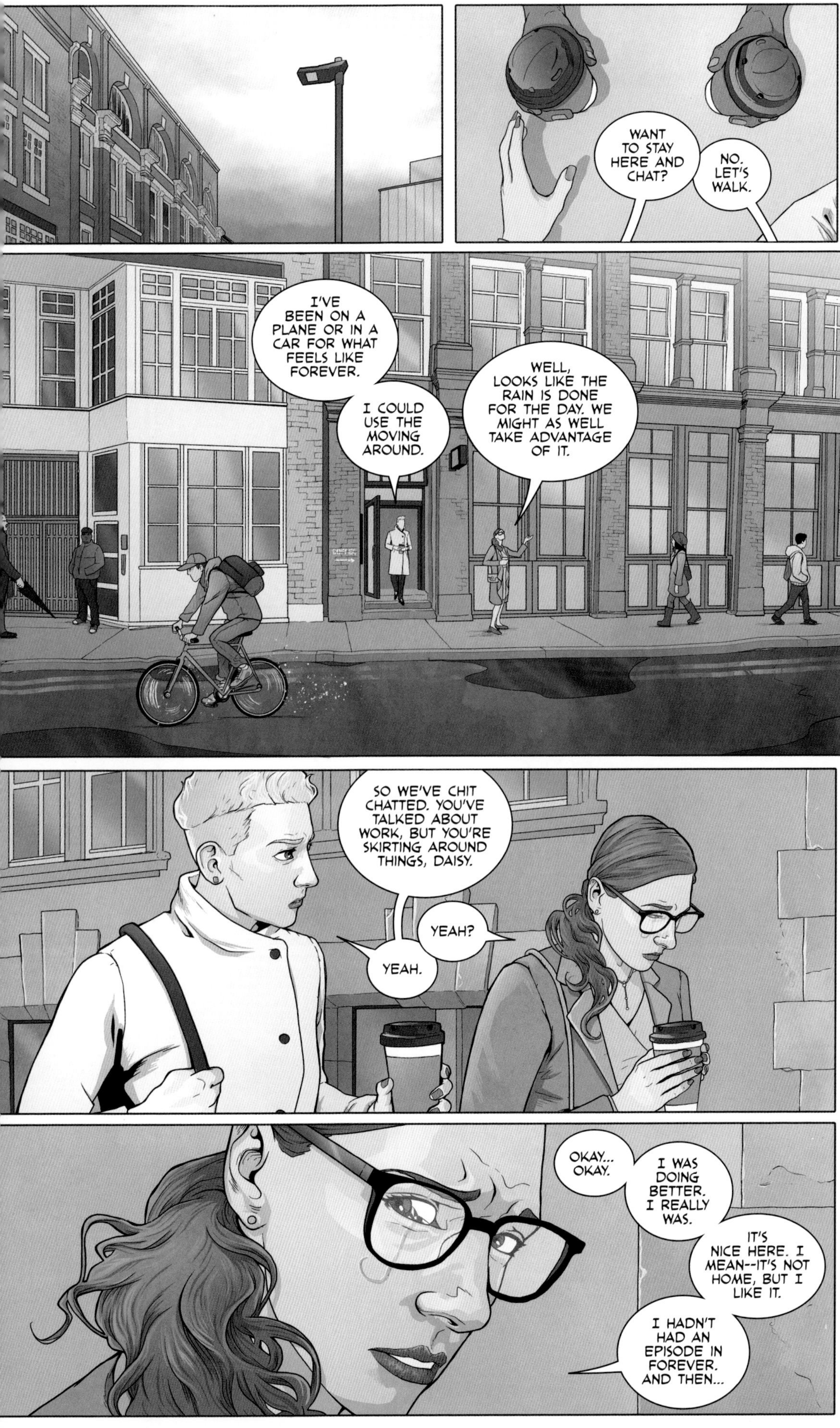
WANT TO STAY HERE AND CHAT?
NO. LET'S WALK.
I'VE BEEN ON A PLANE OR IN A CAR FOR WHAT FEELS LIKE FOREVER.
I COULD USE THE MOVING AROUND.
WELL, LOOKS LIKE THE RAIN IS DONE FOR THE DAY. WE MIGHT AS WELL TAKE ADVANTAGE OF IT.
SO WE'VE CHIT CHATTED. YOU'VE TALKED ABOUT WORK, BUT YOU'RE SKIRTING AROUND THINGS, DAISY.
YEAH?
YEAH.
OKAY... OKAY.
I WAS DOING BETTER. I REALLY WAS.
IT'S NICE HERE. I MEAN--IT'S NOT HOME, BUT I LIKE IT.
I HADN'T HAD AN EPISODE IN FOREVER. AND THEN...

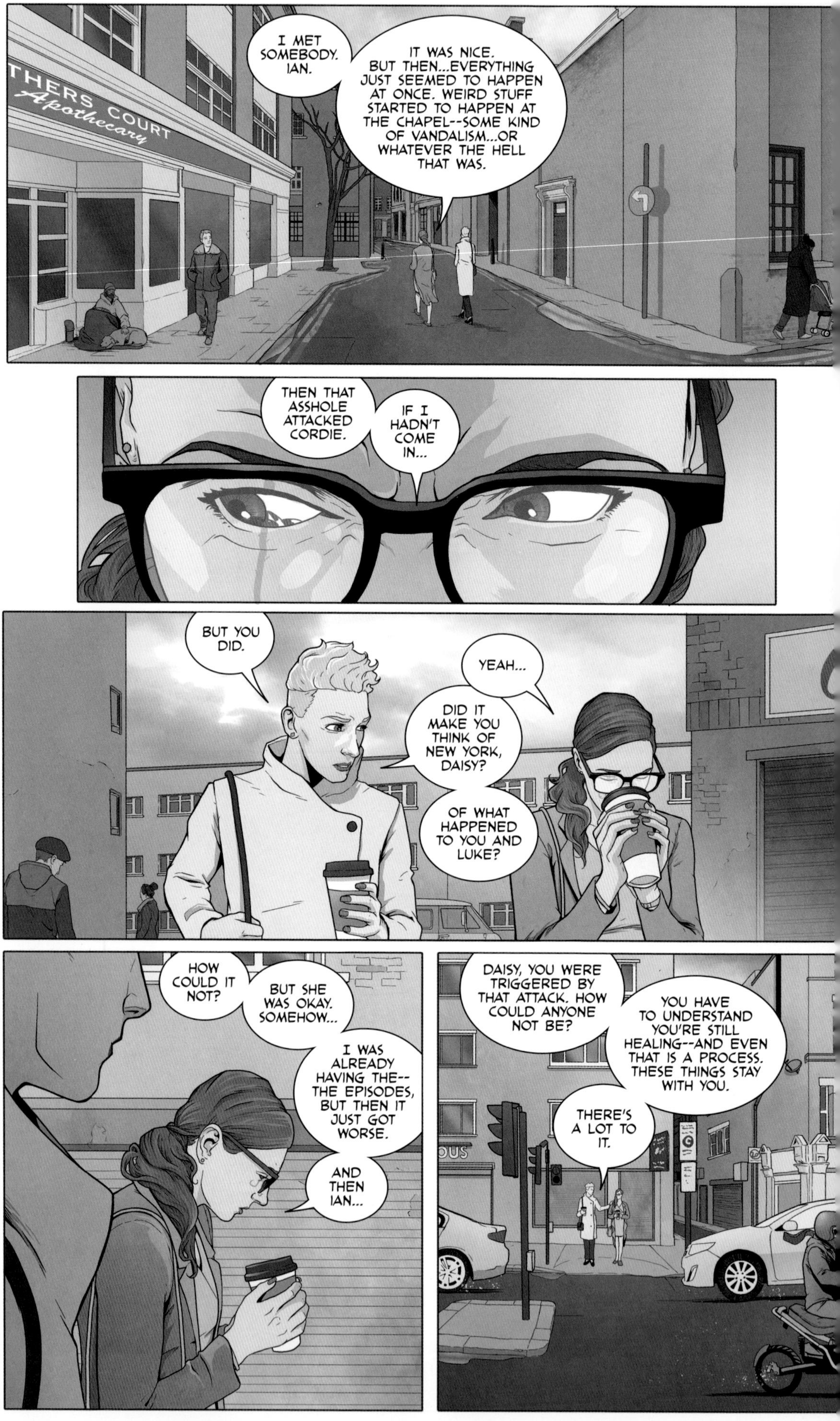
THERS COURT Apothecary
I MET SOMEBODY. IAN.
IT WAS NICE. BUT THEN...EVERYTHING JUST SEEMED TO HAPPEN AT ONCE. WEIRD STUFF STARTED TO HAPPEN AT THE CHAPEL--SOME KIND OF VANDALISM...OR WHATEVER THE HELL THAT WAS.
THEN THAT ASSHOLE ATTACKED CORDIE.
IF I HADN'T COME IN...
BUT YOU DID.
YEAH...
DID IT MAKE YOU THINK OF NEW YORK, DAISY?
OF WHAT HAPPENED TO YOU AND LUKE?
HOW COULD IT NOT?
BUT SHE WAS OKAY. SOMEHOW...
I WAS ALREADY HAVING THE-- THE EPISODES, BUT THEN IT JUST GOT WORSE.
AND THEN IAN...
DAISY, YOU WERE TRIGGERED BY THAT ATTACK. HOW COULD ANYONE NOT BE?
YOU HAVE TO UNDERSTAND YOU'RE STILL HEALING--AND EVEN THAT IS A PROCESS. THESE THINGS STAY WITH YOU.
THERE'S A LOT TO IT.

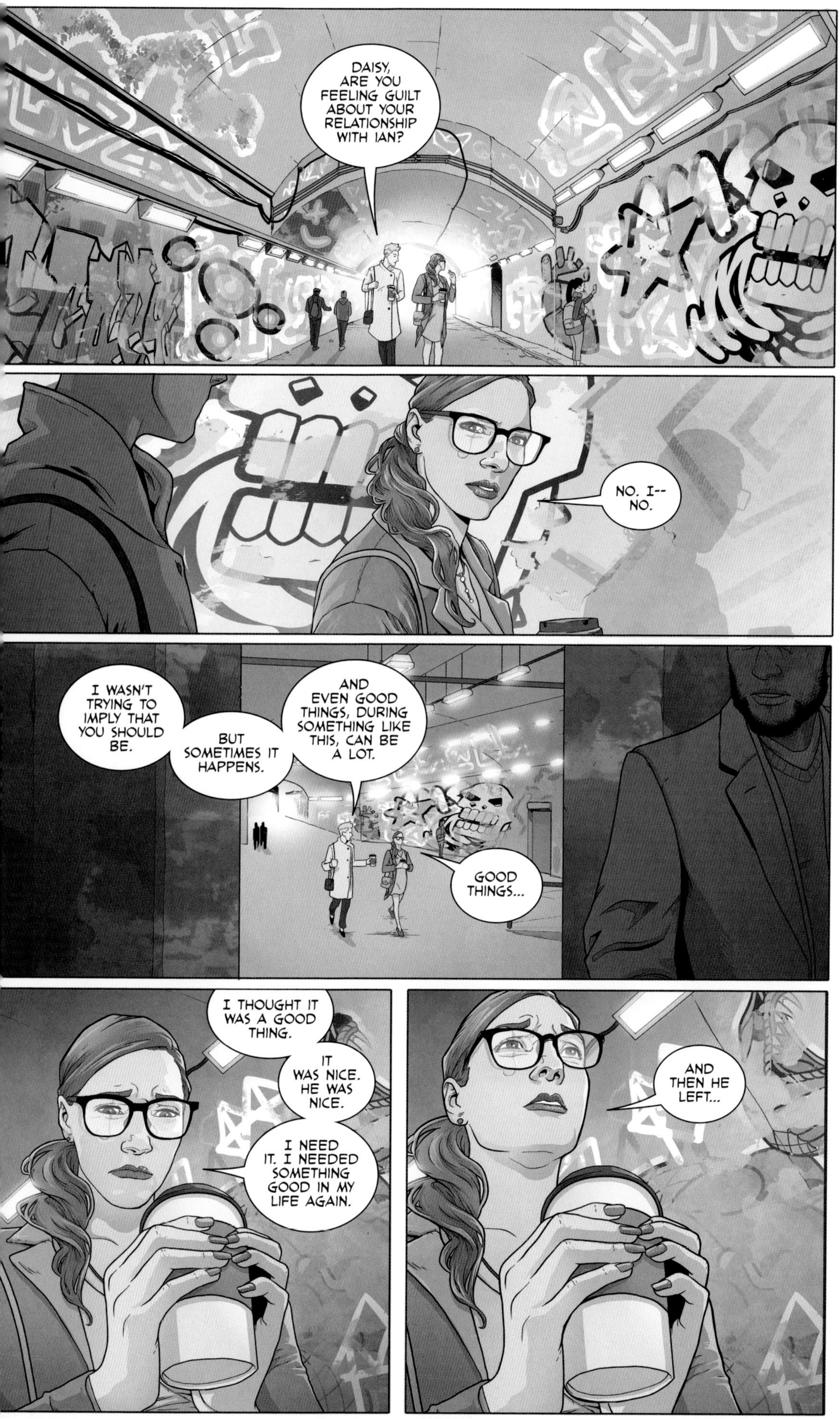
DAISY, ARE YOU FEELING GUILT ABOUT YOUR RELATIONSHIP WITH IAN?
NO. I-- NO.
I WASN'T TRYING TO IMPLY THAT YOU SHOULD BE.
BUT SOMETIMES IT HAPPENS.
AND EVEN GOOD THINGS, DURING SOMETHING LIKE THIS, CAN BE A LOT.
GOOD THINGS...
I THOUGHT IT WAS A GOOD THING.
IT WAS NICE. HE WAS NICE.
I NEED IT. I NEEDED SOMETHING GOOD IN MY LIFE AGAIN.
AND THEN HE LEFT...

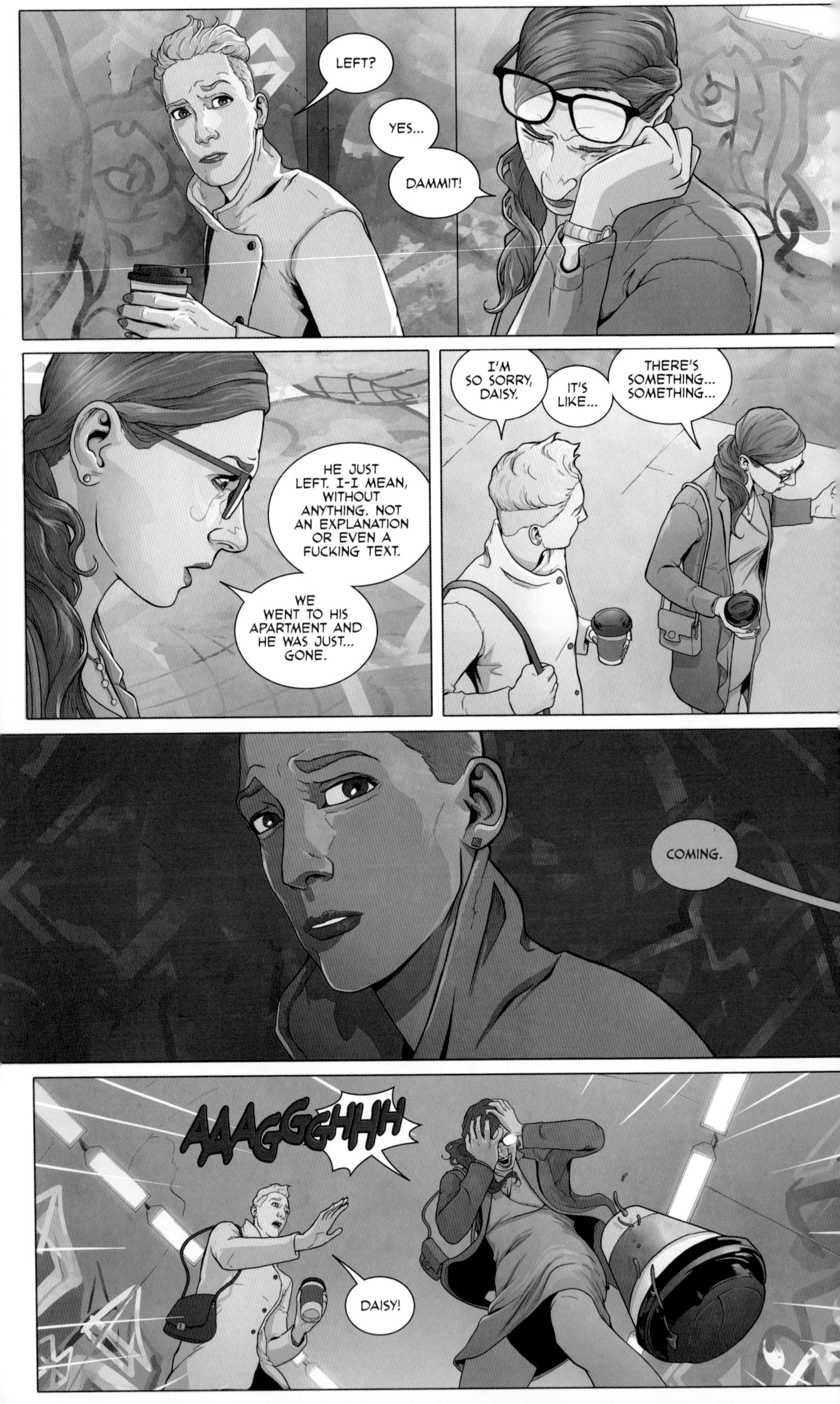
LEFT?
YES...
DAMMIT!
HE JUST LEFT. I-I MEAN, WITHOUT ANYTHING. NOT AN EXPLANATION OR EVEN A FUCKING TEXT.
WE WENT TO HIS APARTMENT AND HE WAS JUST... GONE.
I'M SO SORRY, DAISY.
IT'S LIKE...
THERE'S SOMETHING... SOMETHING...
COMING.
AAAGGGHHH
DAISY!

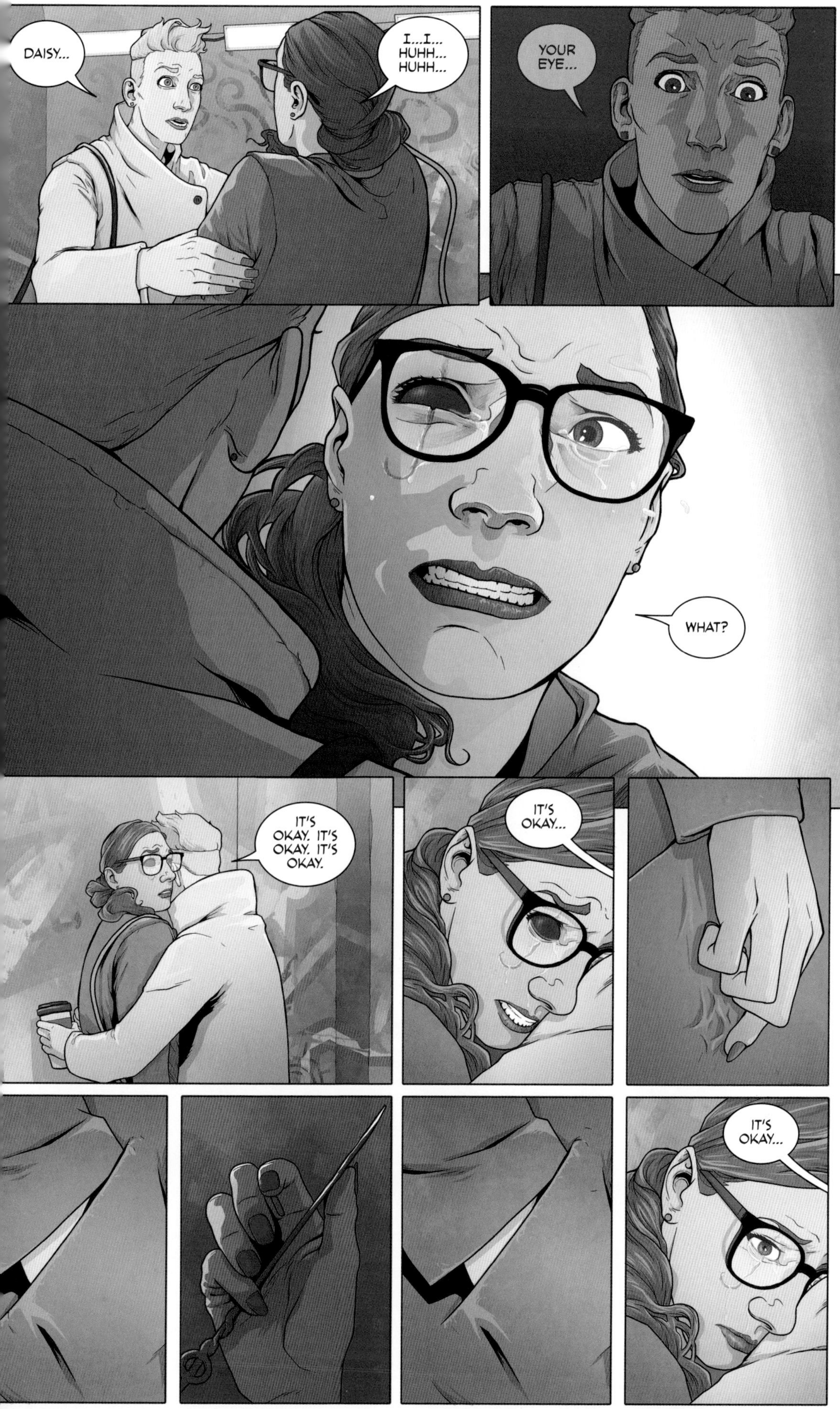
DAISY...
I...I... HUHH... HUHH...
YOUR EYE...
WHAT?
IT'S OKAY. IT'S OKAY. IT'S OKAY.
IT'S OKAY...
IT'S OKAY...

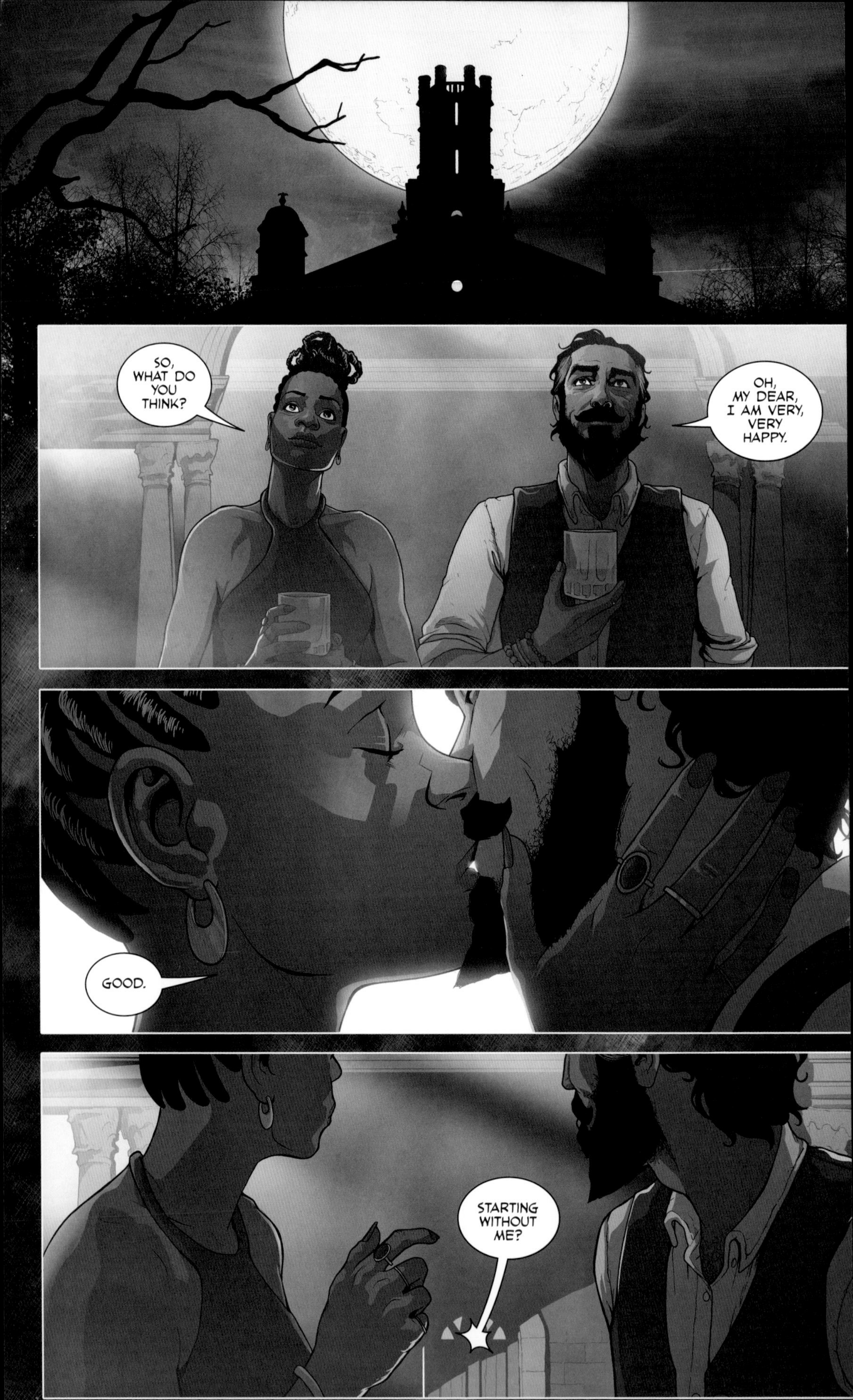
SO, WHAT DO YOU THINK?
OH, MY DEAR, I AM VERY, VERY HAPPY.
GOOD.
STARTING WITHOUT ME?

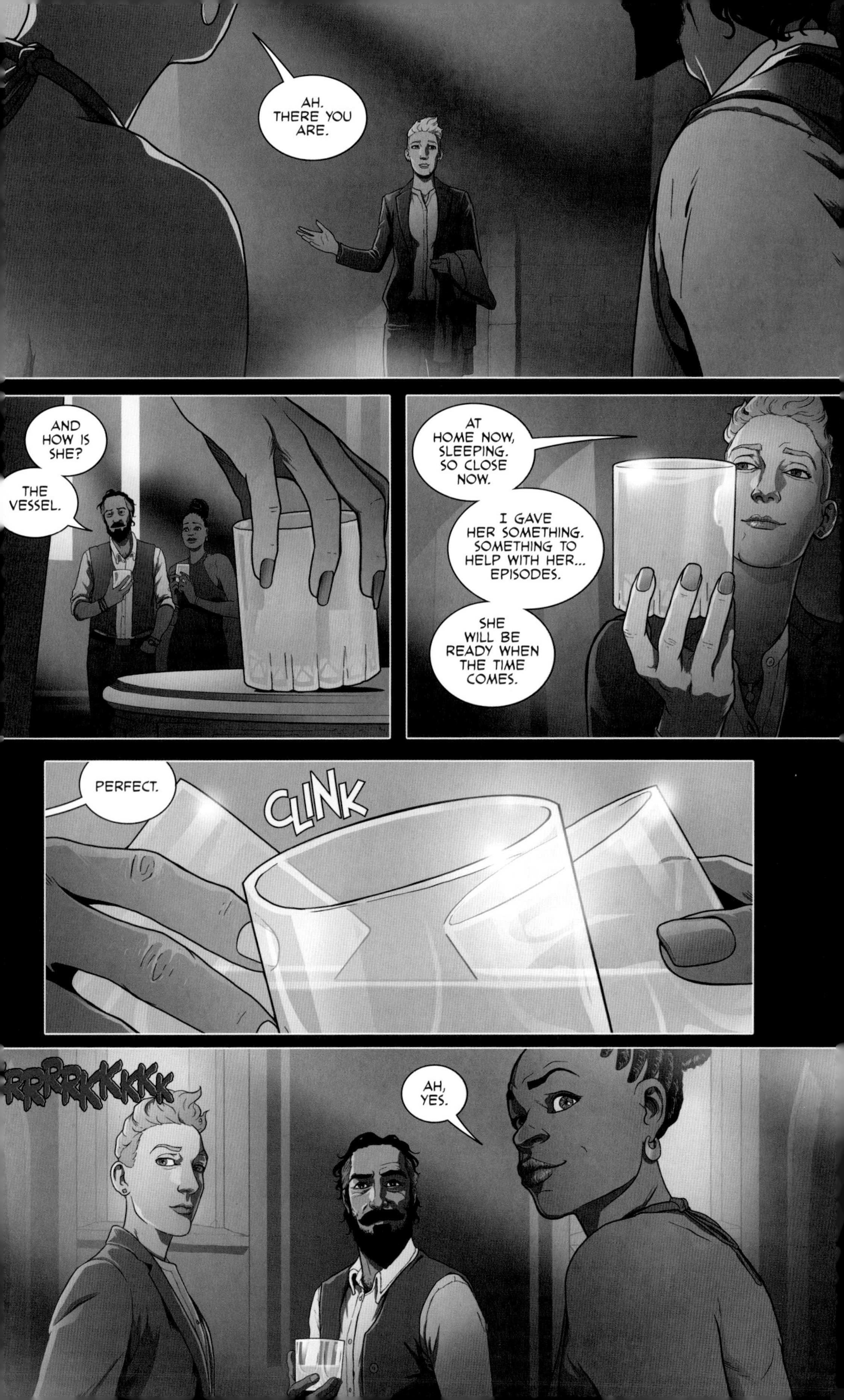
AH. THERE YOU ARE.
AND HOW IS SHE?
THE VESSEL.
AT HOME NOW, SLEEPING. SO CLOSE NOW.
I GAVE HER SOMETHING. SOMETHING TO HELP WITH HER... EPISODES.
SHE WILL BE READY WHEN THE TIME COMES.
PERFECT.
CLINK
RRRRKKKKK
AH, YES.

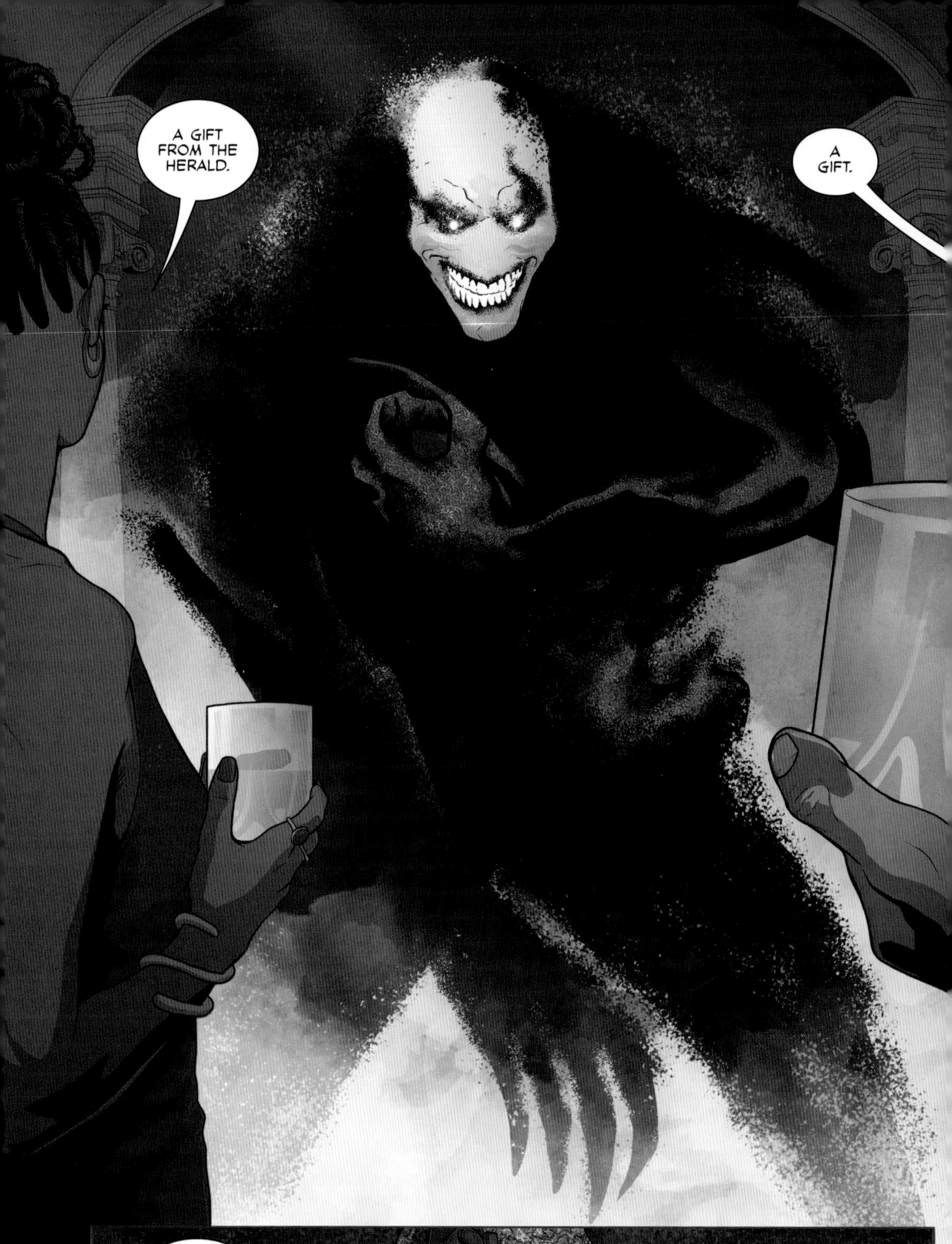
A GIFT FROM THE HERALD.
A GIFT.
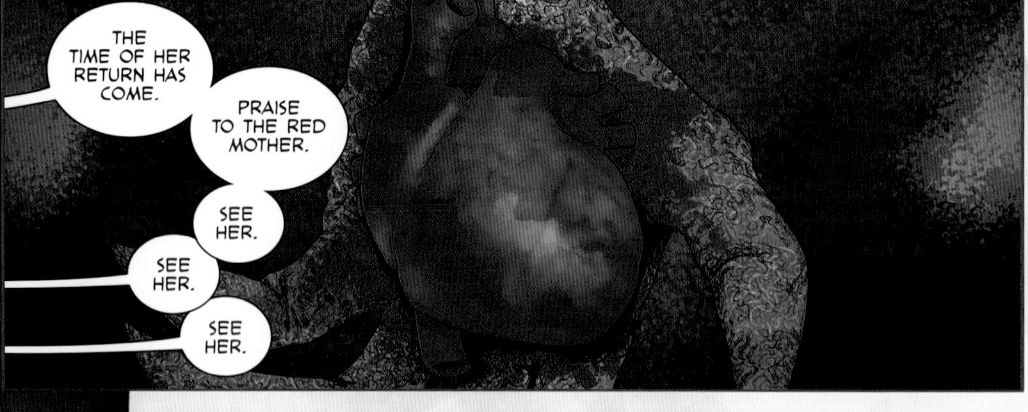
THE TIME OF HER RETURN HAS COME.
PRAISE TO THE RED MOTHER.
SEE HER.
SEE HER.
SEE HER.

CHAPTER ELEVEN

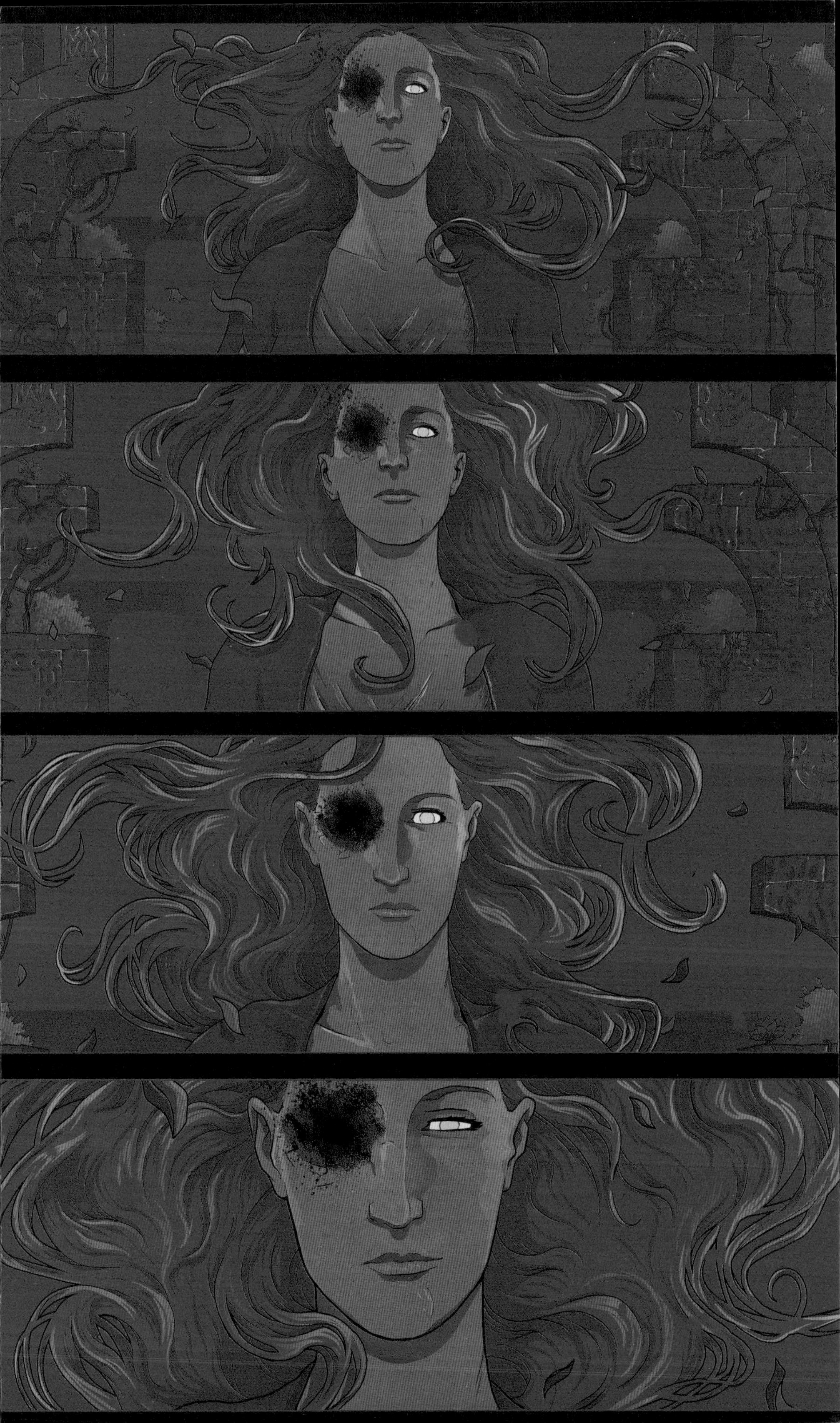

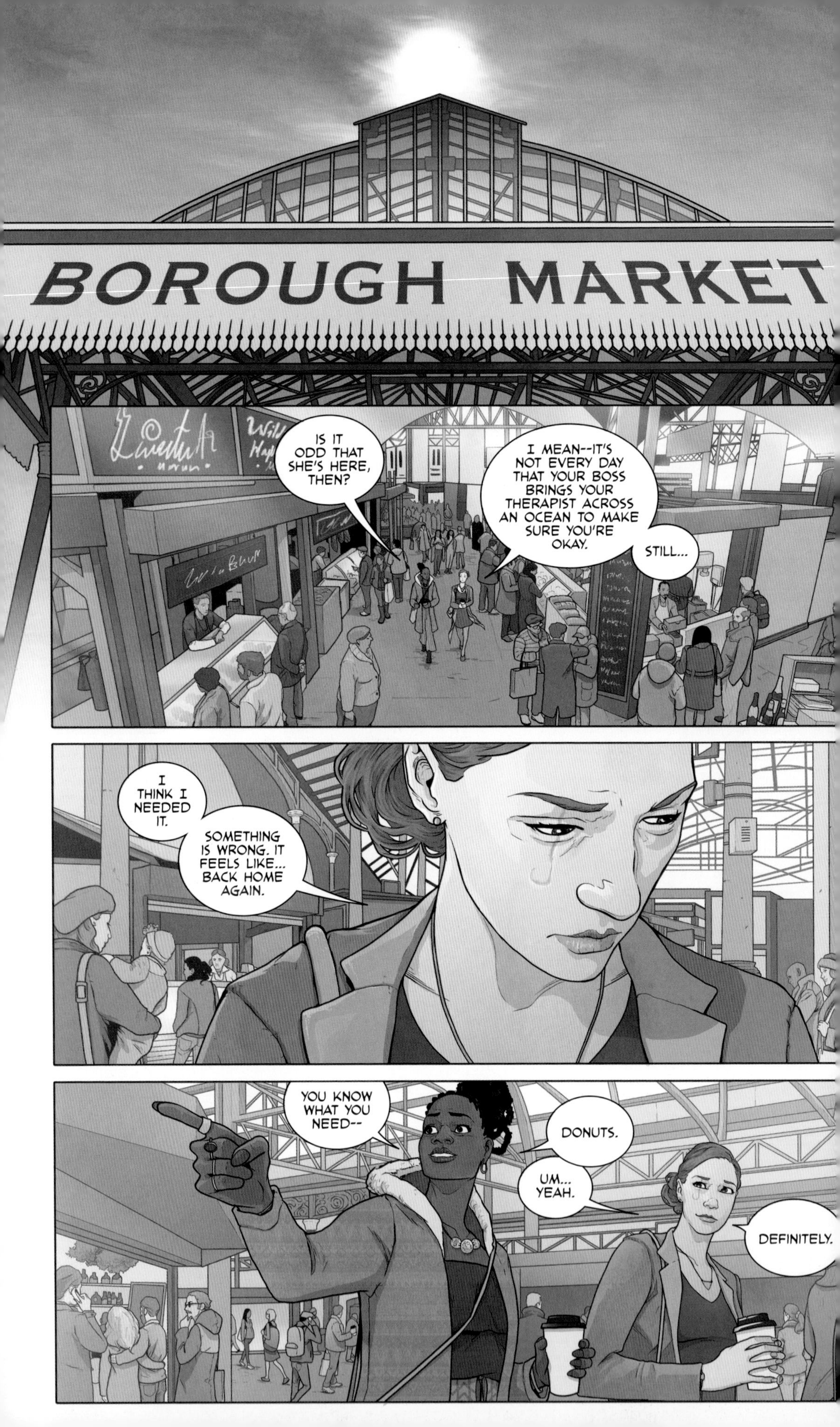
BOROUGH MARKET
IS IT ODD THAT SHE'S HERE, THEN?
I MEAN--IT'S NOT EVERY DAY THAT YOUR BOSS BRINGS YOUR THERAPIST ACROSS AN OCEAN TO MAKE SURE YOU'RE OKAY.
STILL...
I THINK I NEEDED IT.
SOMETHING IS WRONG. IT FEELS LIKE... BACK HOME AGAIN.
YOU KNOW WHAT YOU NEED--
DONUTS.
UM... YEAH.
DEFINITELY.

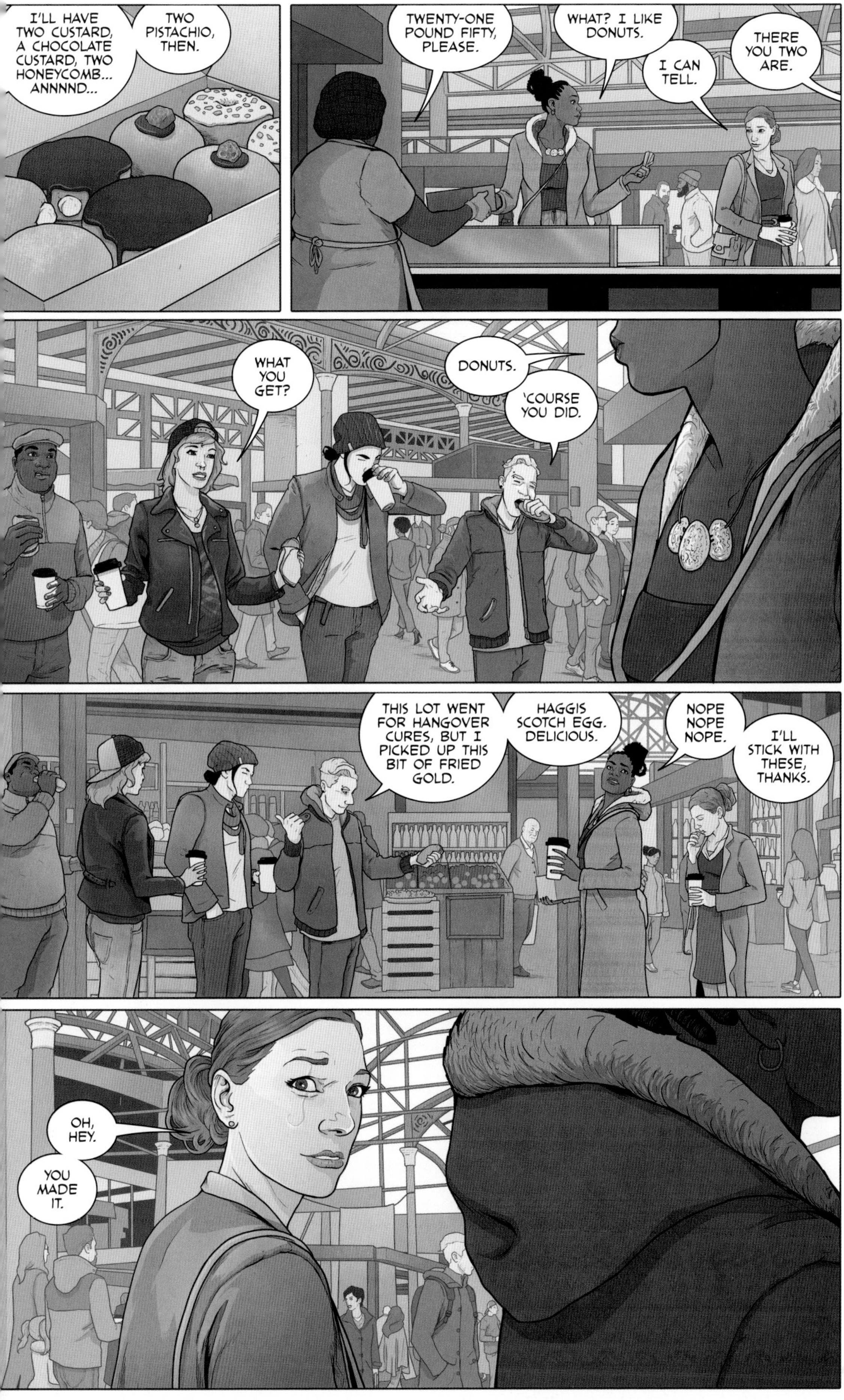

I'LL HAVE TWO CUSTARD, A CHOCOLATE CUSTARD, TWO HONEYCOMB... ANNNND...
TWO PISTACHIO, THEN.
TWENTY-ONE POUND FIFTY, PLEASE.
WHAT? I LIKE DONUTS.
I CAN TELL.
THERE YOU TWO ARE.
WHAT YOU GET?
DONUTS.
'COURSE YOU DID.
THIS LOT WENT FOR HANGOVER CURES, BUT I PICKED UP THIS BIT OF FRIED GOLD.
HAGGIS SCOTCH EGG. DELICIOUS.
NOPE NOPE NOPE.
I'LL STICK WITH THESE, THANKS.
OH, HEY.
YOU MADE IT.

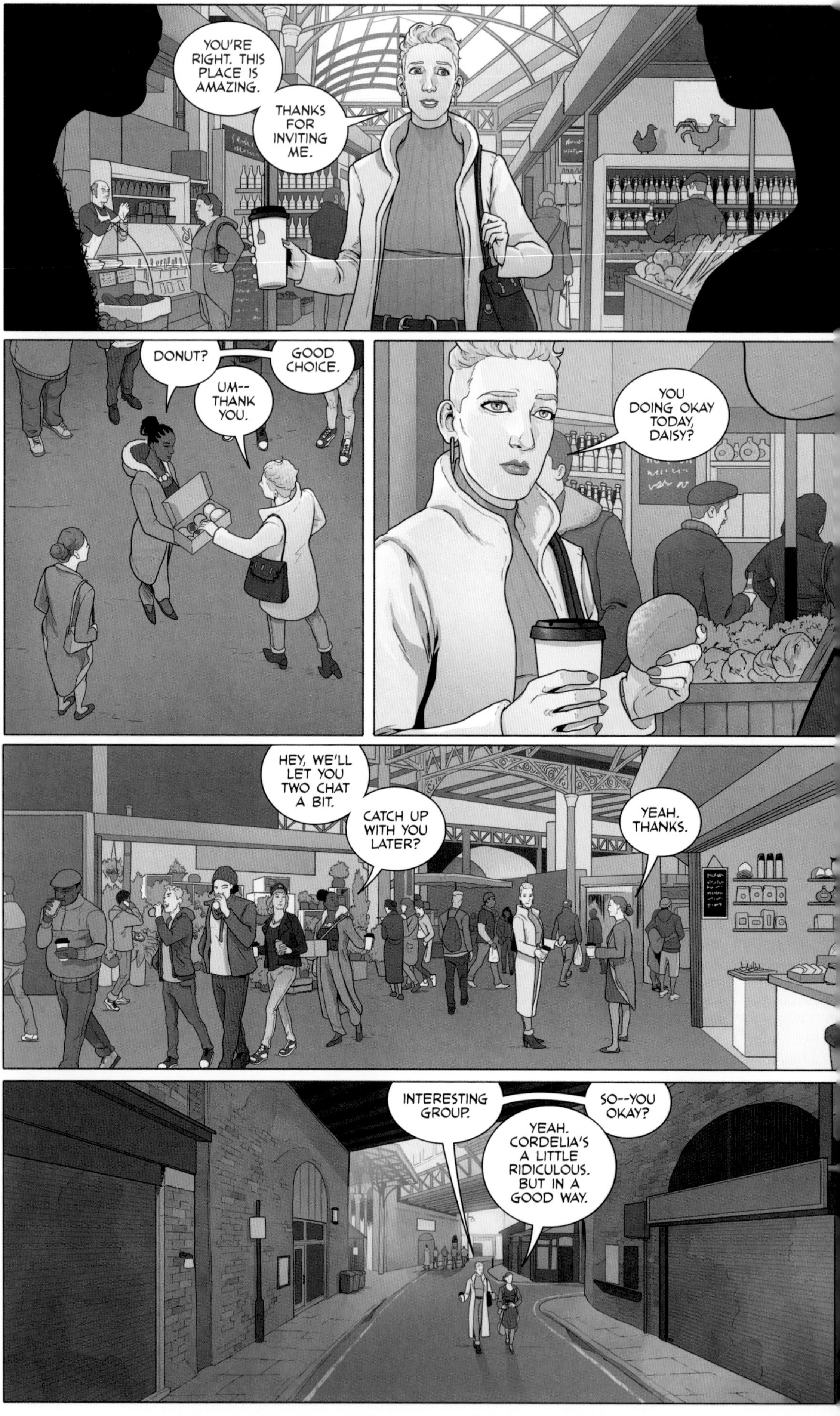
YOU'RE RIGHT. THIS PLACE IS AMAZING.
THANKS FOR INVITING ME.
DONUT?
GOOD CHOICE.
UM-- THANK YOU.
YOU DOING OKAY TODAY, DAISY?
HEY, WE'LL LET YOU TWO CHAT A BIT.
CATCH UP WITH YOU LATER?
YEAH. THANKS.
INTERESTING GROUP.
SO--YOU OKAY?
YEAH. CORDELIA'S A LITTLE RIDICULOUS. BUT IN A GOOD WAY.

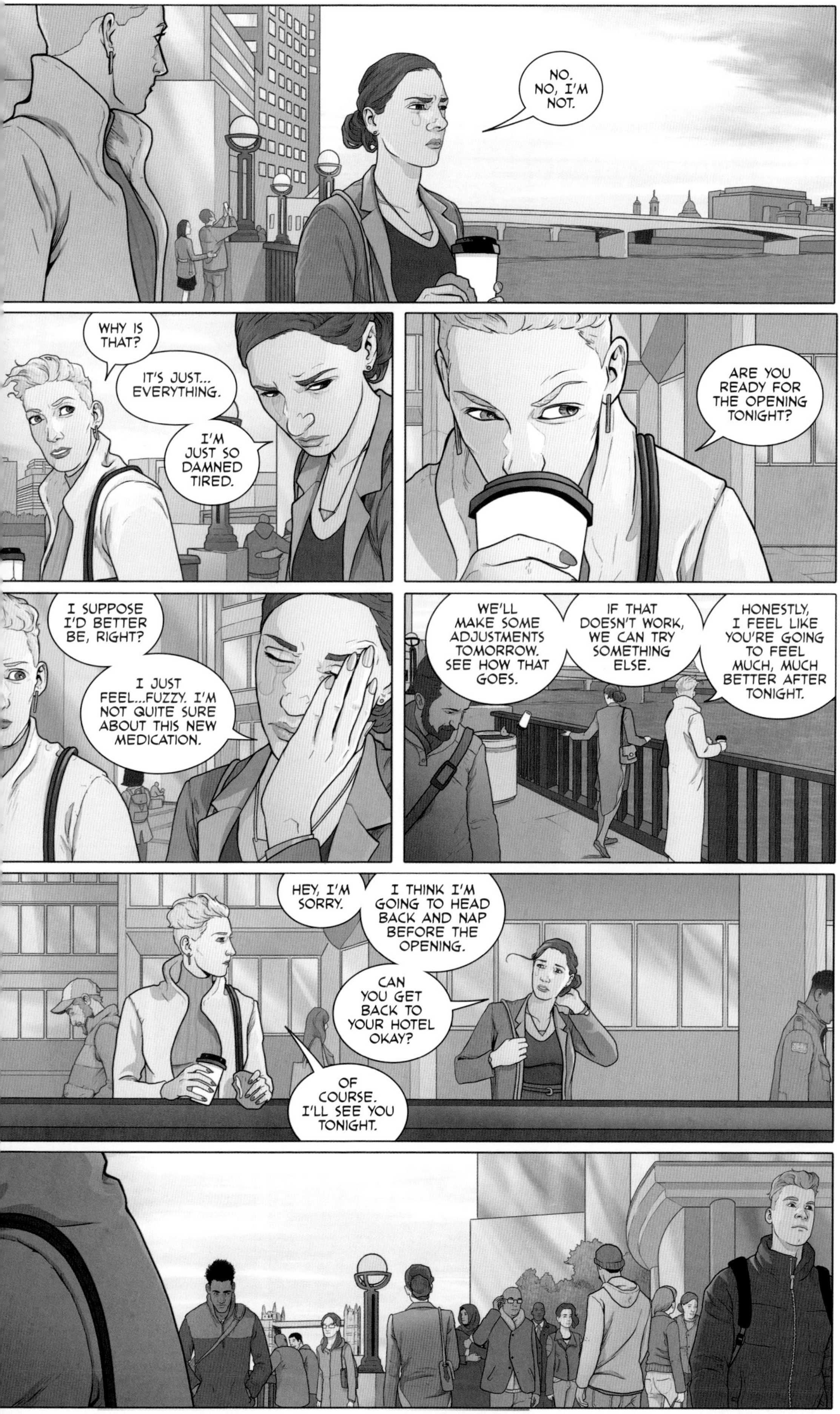
NO. NO, I'M NOT.
WHY IS THAT?
IT'S JUST... EVERYTHING.
I'M JUST SO DAMNED TIRED.
ARE YOU READY FOR THE OPENING TONIGHT?
I SUPPOSE I'D BETTER BE, RIGHT?
I JUST FEEL...FUZZY. I'M NOT QUITE SURE ABOUT THIS NEW MEDICATION.
WE'LL MAKE SOME ADJUSTMENTS TOMORROW. SEE HOW THAT GOES.
IF THAT DOESN'T WORK, WE CAN TRY SOMETHING ELSE.
HONESTLY, I FEEL LIKE YOU'RE GOING TO FEEL MUCH, MUCH BETTER AFTER TONIGHT.
HEY, I'M SORRY.
I THINK I'M GOING TO HEAD BACK AND NAP BEFORE THE OPENING.
CAN YOU GET BACK TO YOUR HOTEL OKAY?
OF COURSE. I'LL SEE YOU TONIGHT.

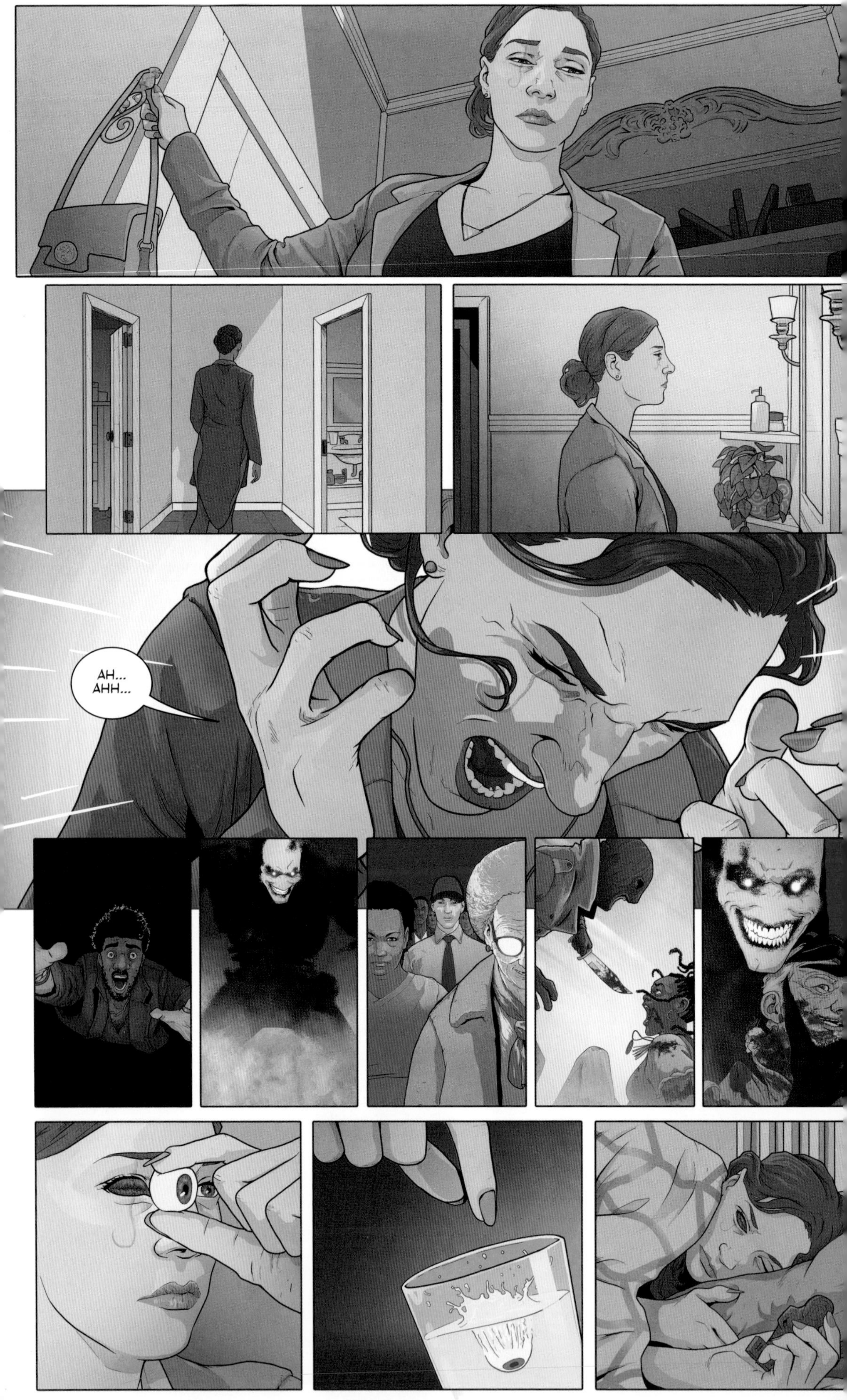
AH...
AHH...

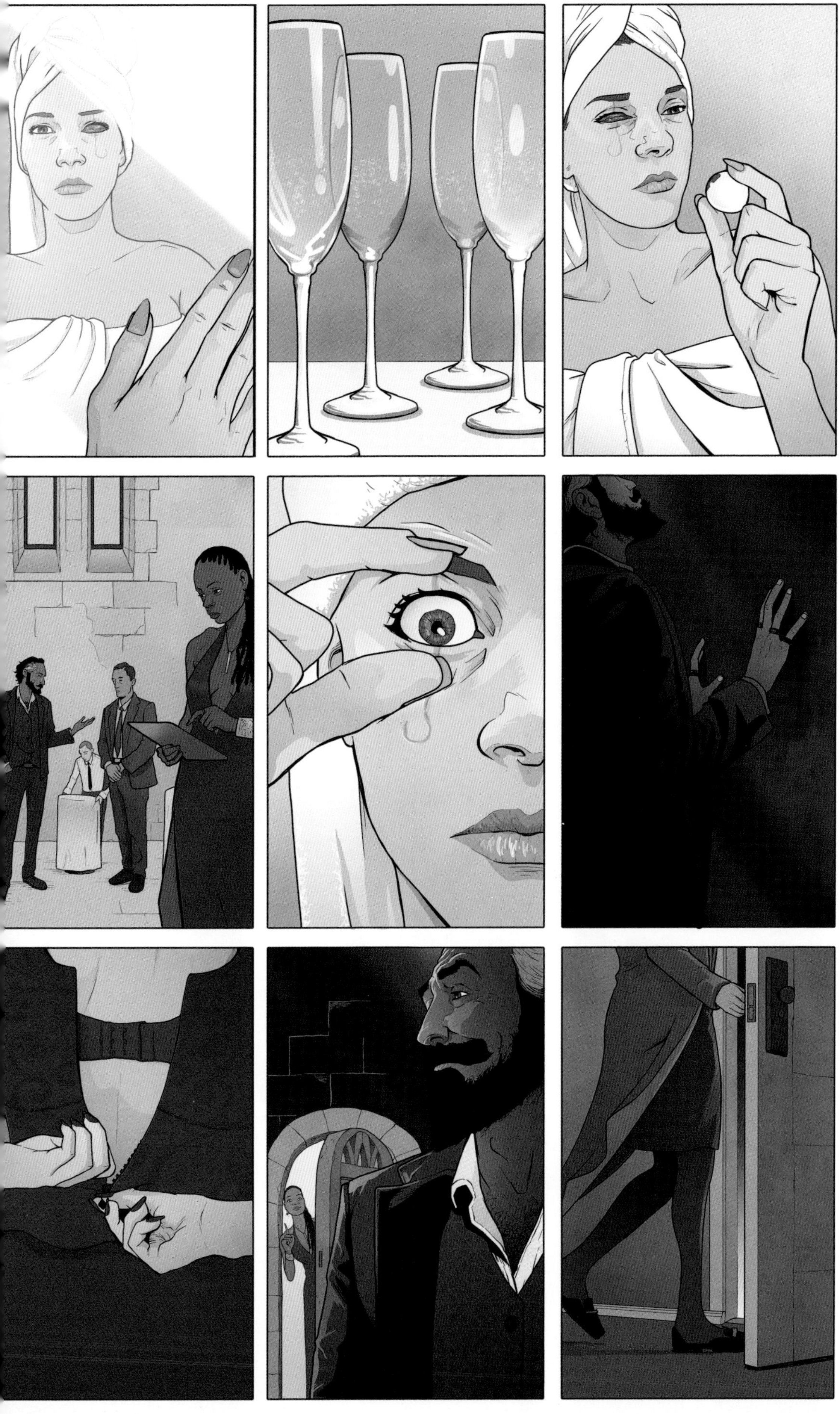

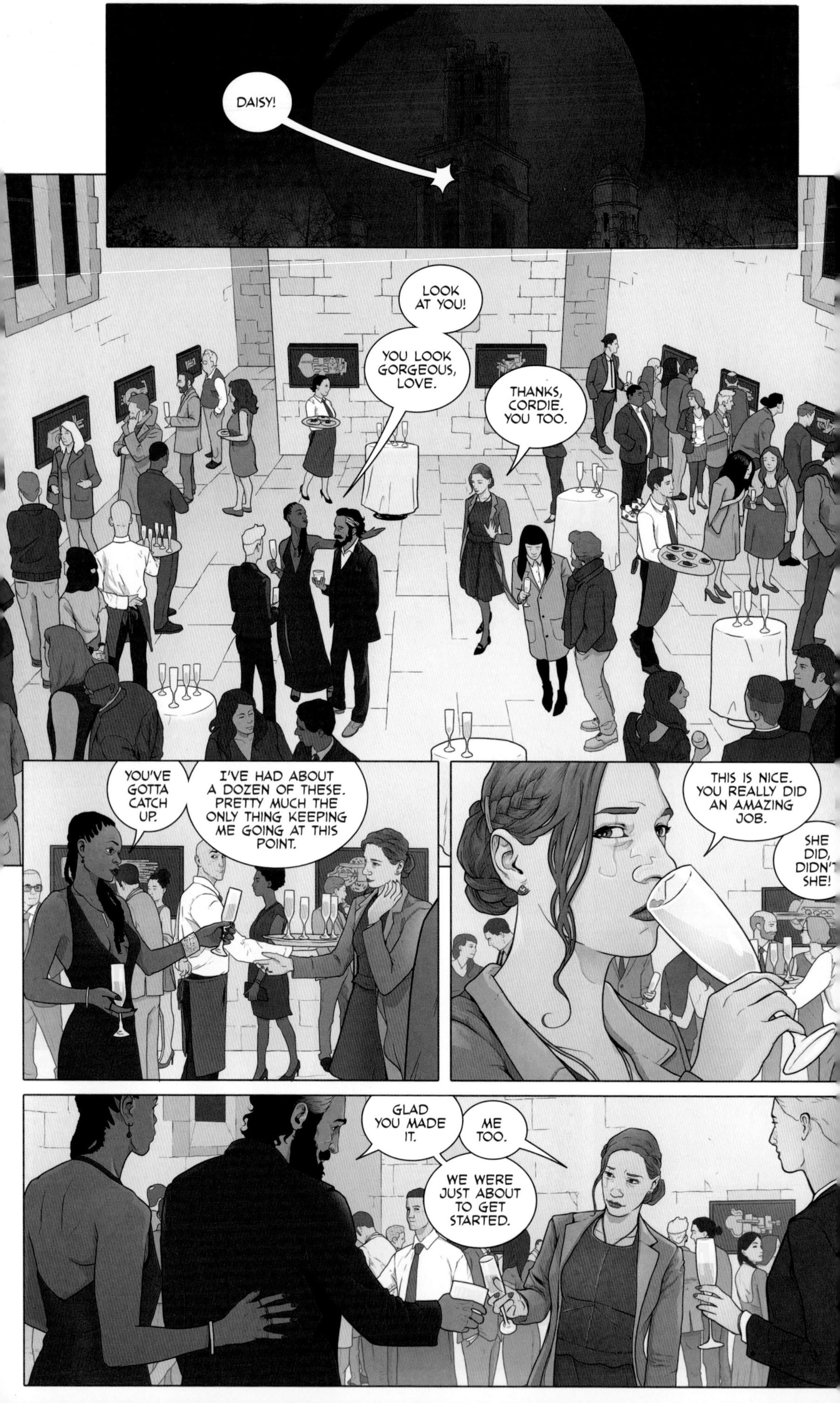
DAISY!
LOOK AT YOU!
YOU LOOK GORGEOUS, LOVE.
THANKS, CORDIE. YOU TOO.
YOU'VE GOTTA CATCH UP.
I'VE HAD ABOUT A DOZEN OF THESE. PRETTY MUCH THE ONLY THING KEEPING ME GOING AT THIS POINT.
THIS IS NICE. YOU REALLY DID AN AMAZING JOB.
SHE DID, DIDN'T SHE!
GLAD YOU MADE IT.
ME TOO.
WE WERE JUST ABOUT TO GET STARTED.

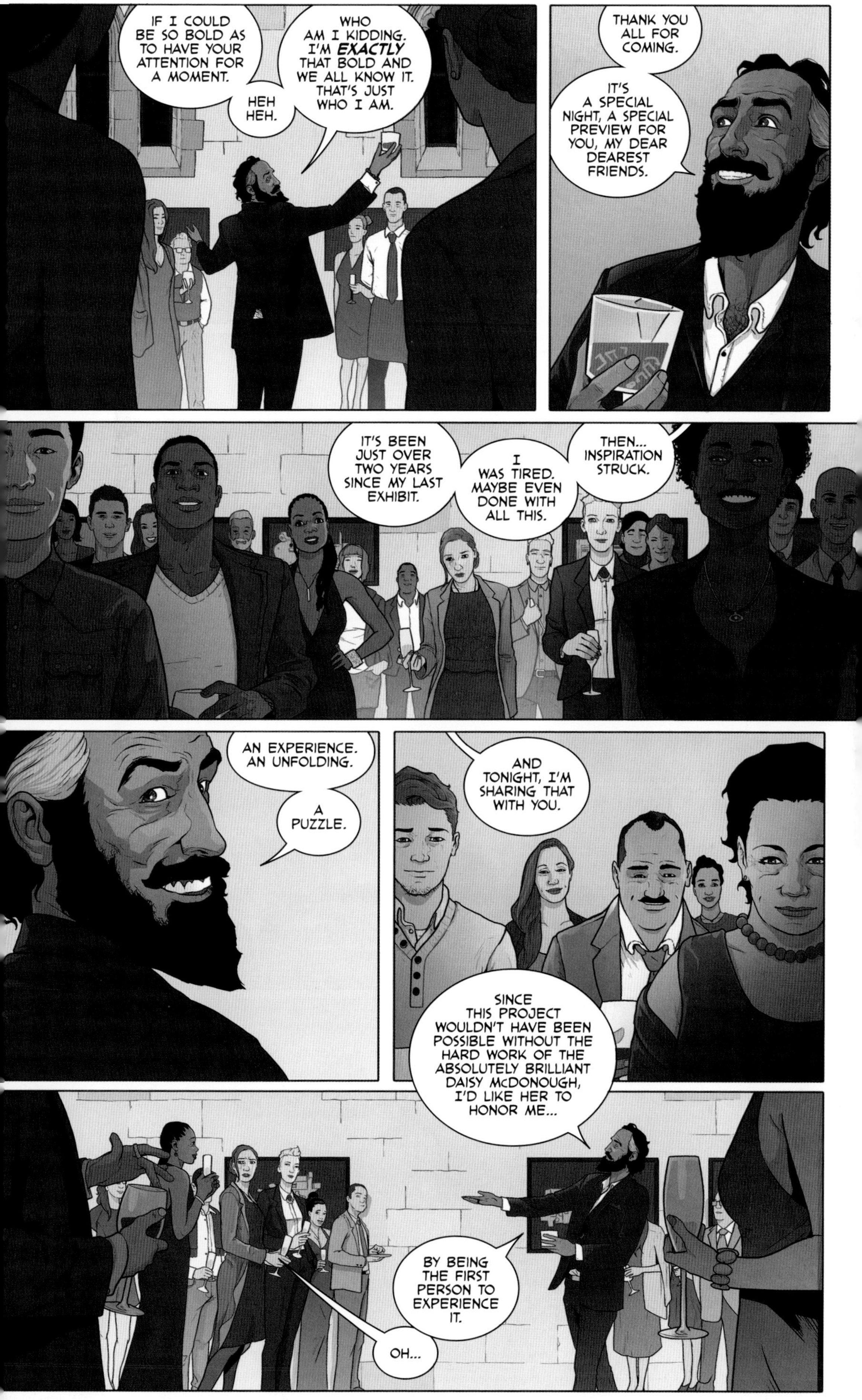
IF I COULD BE SO BOLD AS TO HAVE YOUR ATTENTION FOR A MOMENT.
HEH HEH.
WHO AM I KIDDING. I'M ***EXACTLY*** THAT BOLD AND WE ALL KNOW IT. THAT'S JUST WHO I AM.
THANK YOU ALL FOR COMING.
IT'S A SPECIAL NIGHT, A SPECIAL PREVIEW FOR YOU, MY DEAR DEAREST FRIENDS.
IT'S BEEN JUST OVER TWO YEARS SINCE MY LAST EXHIBIT.
I WAS TIRED. MAYBE EVEN DONE WITH ALL THIS.
THEN... INSPIRATION STRUCK.
AN EXPERIENCE. AN UNFOLDING.
A PUZZLE.
AND TONIGHT, I'M SHARING THAT WITH YOU.
SINCE THIS PROJECT WOULDN'T HAVE BEEN POSSIBLE WITHOUT THE HARD WORK OF THE ABSOLUTELY BRILLIANT DAISY McDONOUGH, I'D LIKE HER TO HONOR ME...
BY BEING THE FIRST PERSON TO EXPERIENCE IT.
OH...

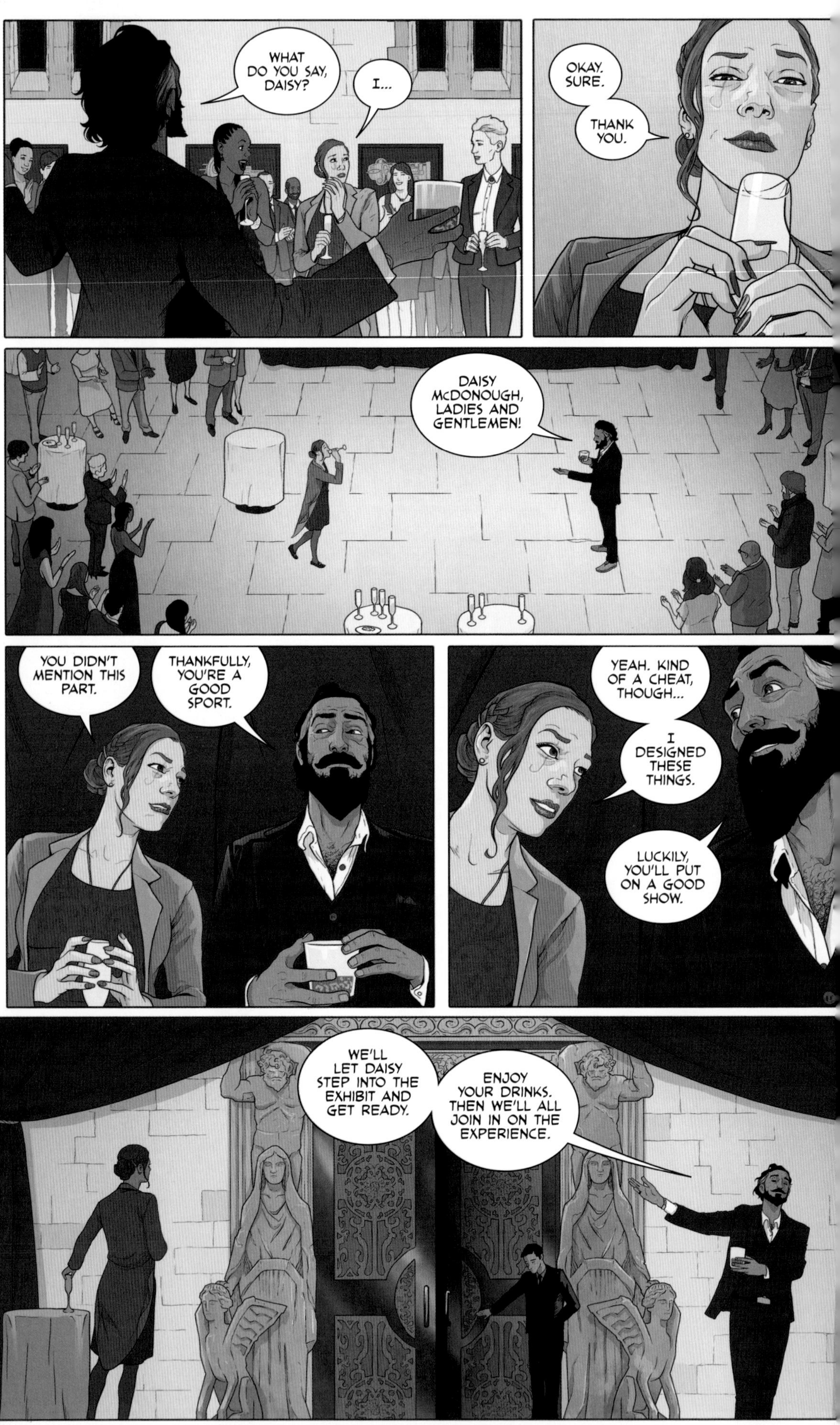
WHAT DO YOU SAY, DAISY?
I...
OKAY. SURE.
THANK YOU.
DAISY McDONOUGH, LADIES AND GENTLEMEN!
YOU DIDN'T MENTION THIS PART.
THANKFULLY, YOU'RE A GOOD SPORT.
YEAH. KIND OF A CHEAT, THOUGH...
I DESIGNED THESE THINGS.
LUCKILY, YOU'LL PUT ON A GOOD SHOW.
WE'LL LET DAISY STEP INTO THE EXHIBIT AND GET READY.
ENJOY YOUR DRINKS. THEN WE'LL ALL JOIN IN ON THE EXPERIENCE.

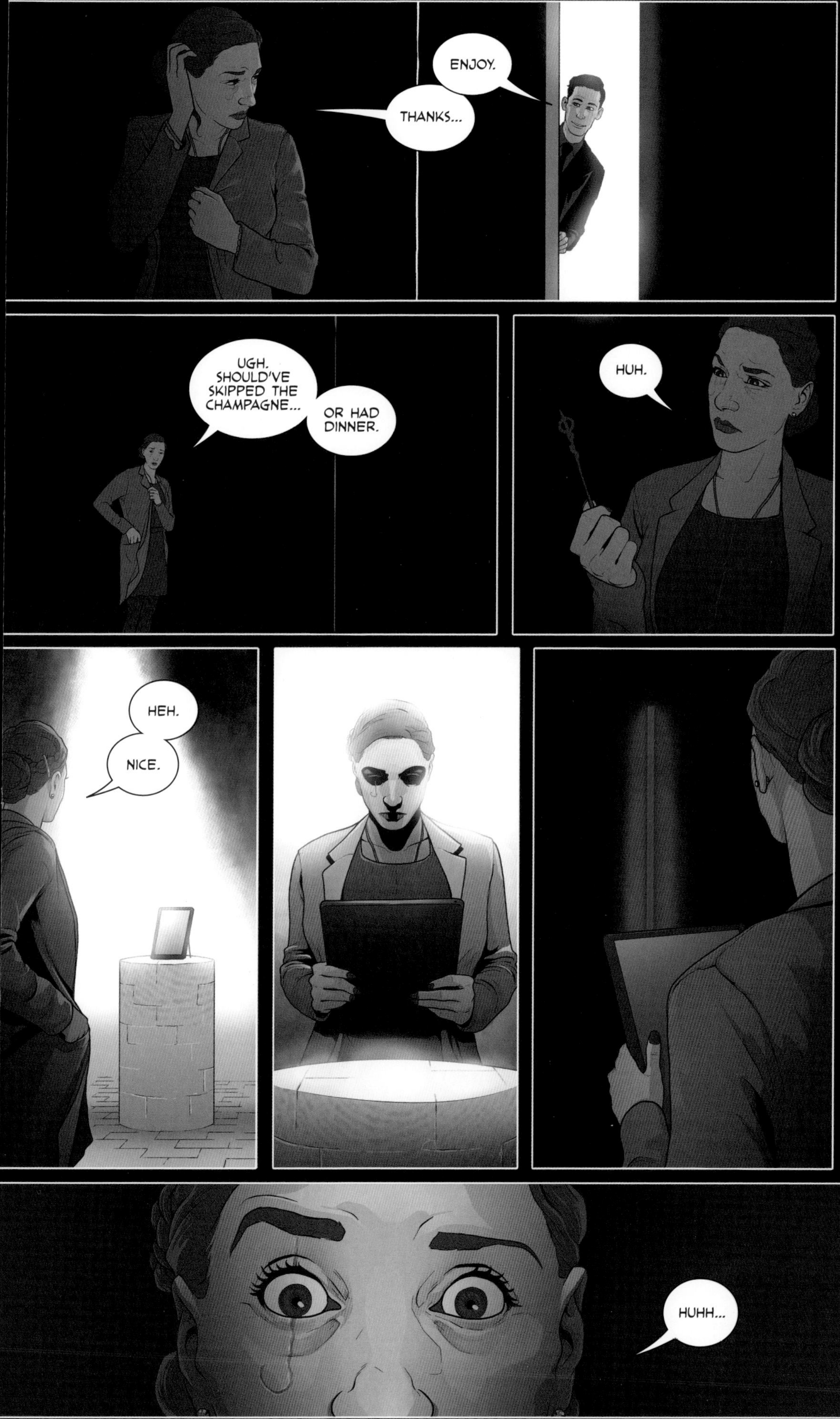
ENJOY.
THANKS...
UGH. SHOULD'VE SKIPPED THE CHAMPAGNE...
OR HAD DINNER.
HUH.
HEH.
NICE.
HUHH...

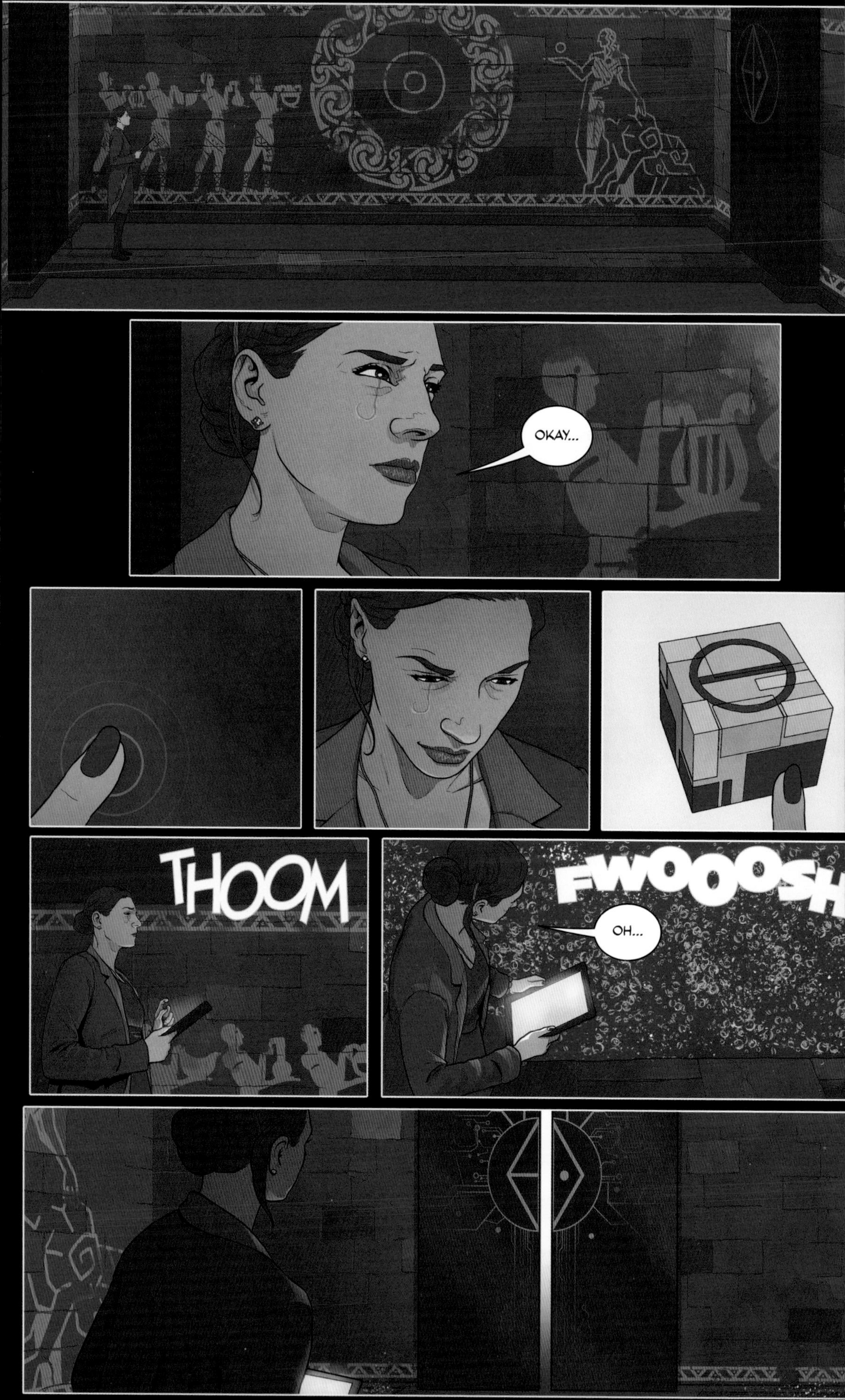
OKAY...
THOOM
FWOOOSH
OH...

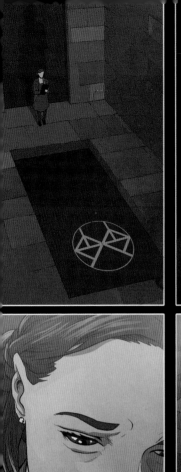

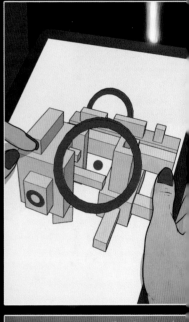

OH...

THUM
THUM
THUM

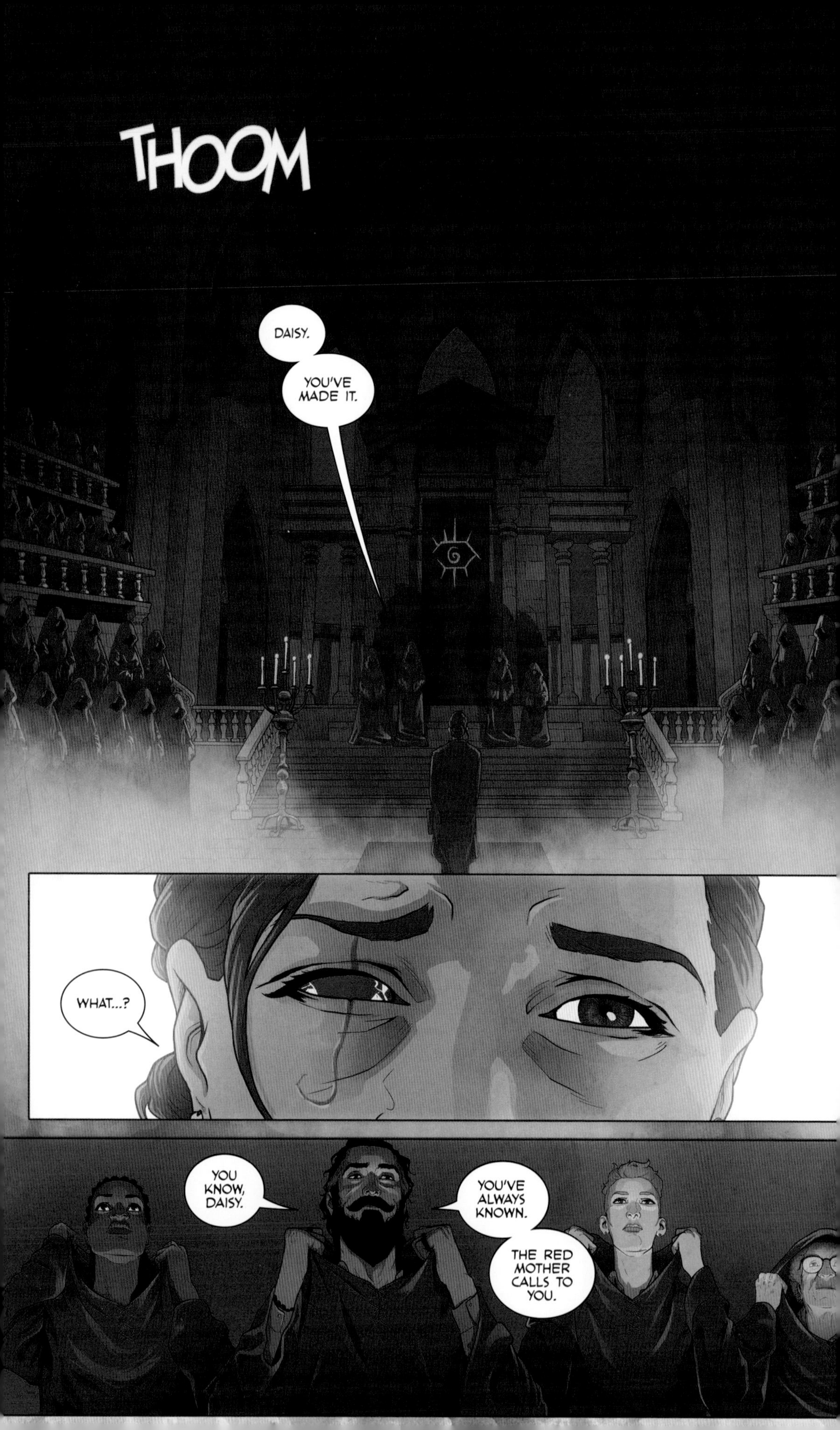
THOOM
DAISY.
YOU'VE MADE IT.
WHAT...?
YOU KNOW, DAISY.
YOU'VE ALWAYS KNOWN.
THE RED MOTHER CALLS TO YOU.

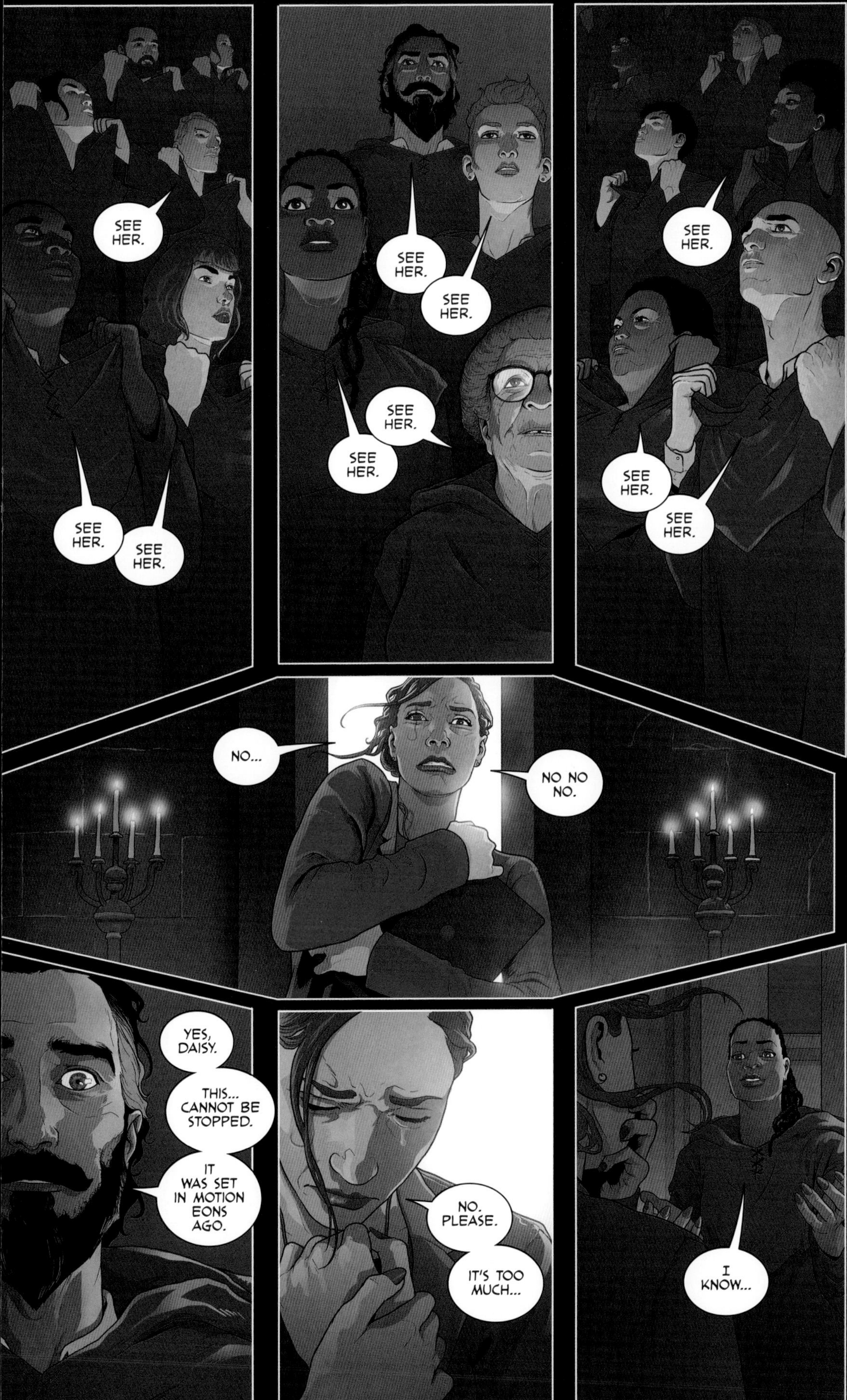
SEE HER.
SEE HER.
SEE HER.
SEE HER.
SEE HER.
SEE HER.
SEE HER.
SEE HER.
SEE HER.
SEE HER.
NO...
NO NO NO.
YES, DAISY.
THIS... CANNOT BE STOPPED.
IT WAS SET IN MOTION EONS AGO.
NO. PLEASE.
IT'S TOO MUCH...
I KNOW...

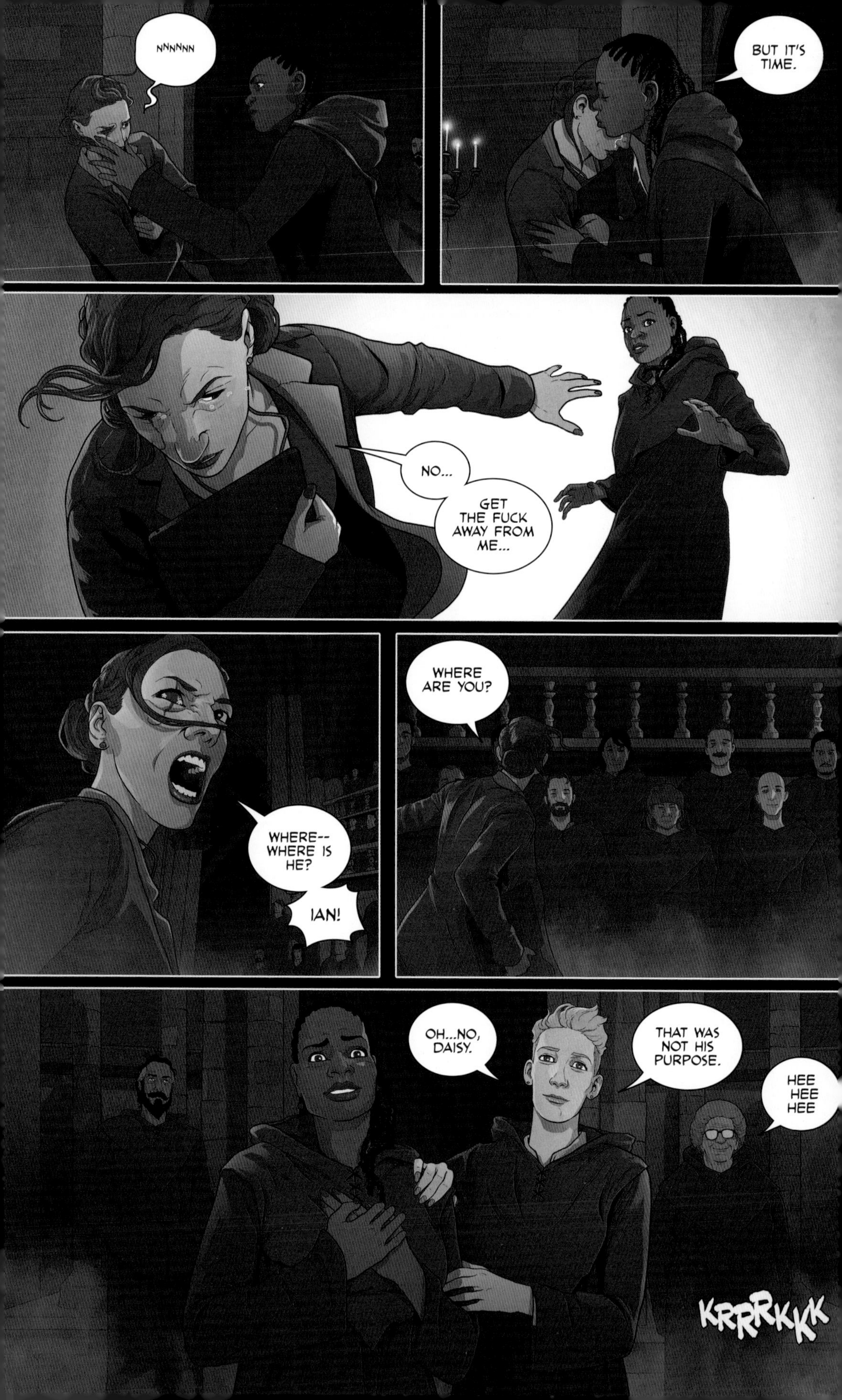
NNNNNN
BUT IT'S TIME.
NO...
GET THE FUCK AWAY FROM ME...
WHERE-- WHERE IS HE?
IAN!
WHERE ARE YOU?
OH...NO, DAISY.
THAT WAS NOT HIS PURPOSE.
HEE HEE HEE
KRRRKKK

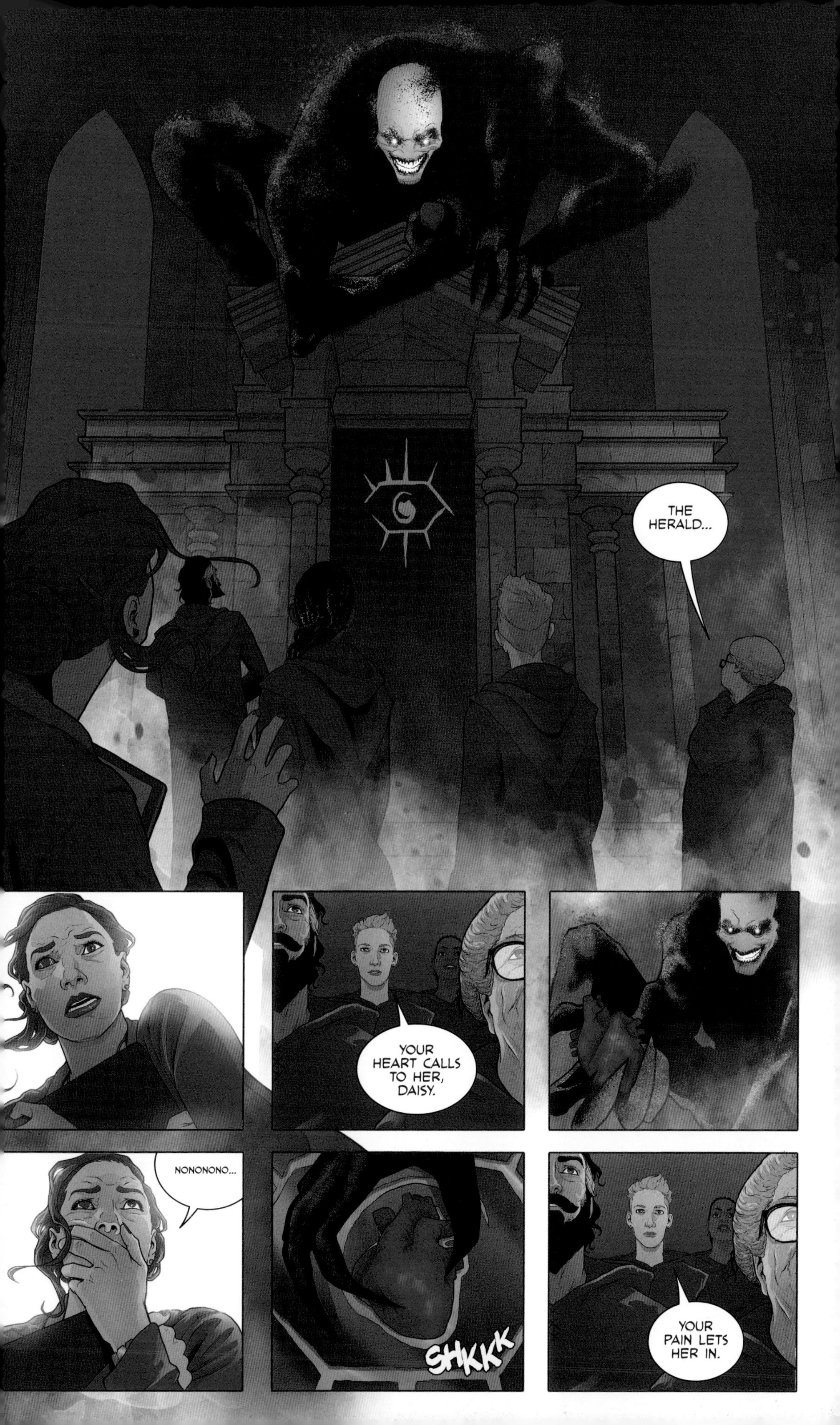
THE HERALD...
YOUR HEART CALLS TO HER, DAISY.
NONONONO...
SHKKK
YOUR PAIN LETS HER IN.

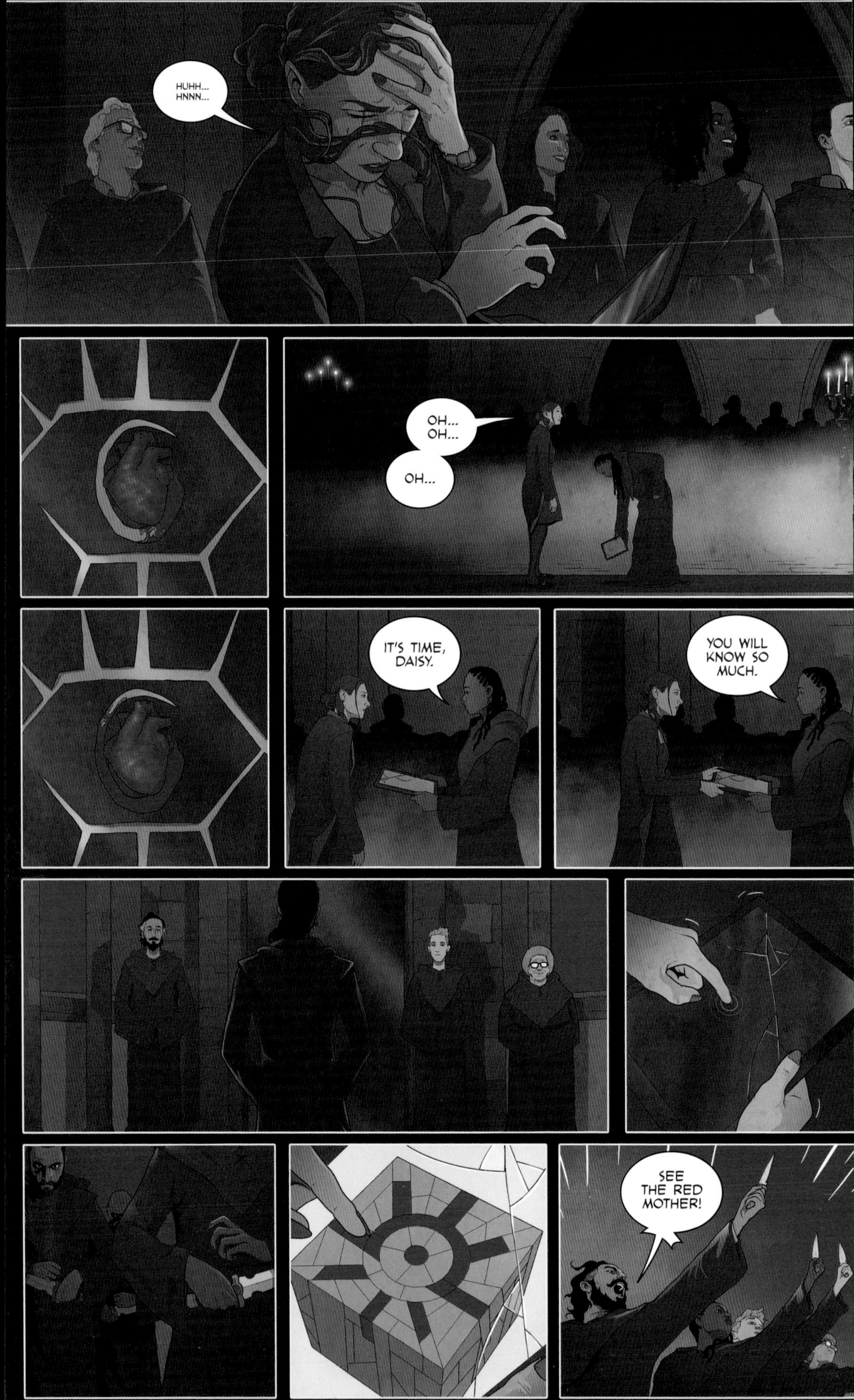
HUHH...
HNNN...
OH...
OH...
OH...
IT'S TIME, DAISY.
YOU WILL KNOW SO MUCH.
SEE THE RED MOTHER!

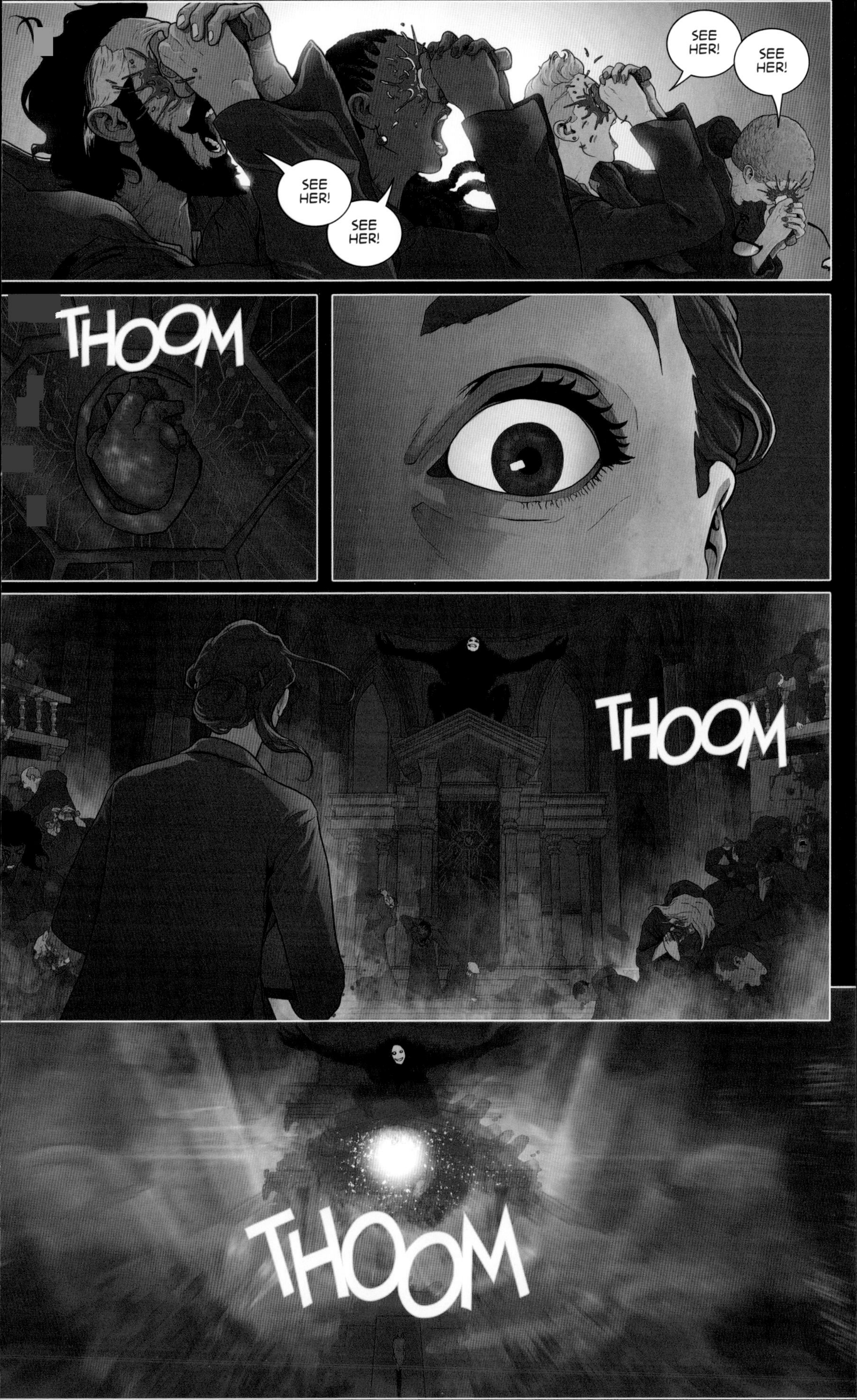
SEE HER!
SEE HER!
SEE HER!
SEE HER!
THOOM
THOOM
THOOM

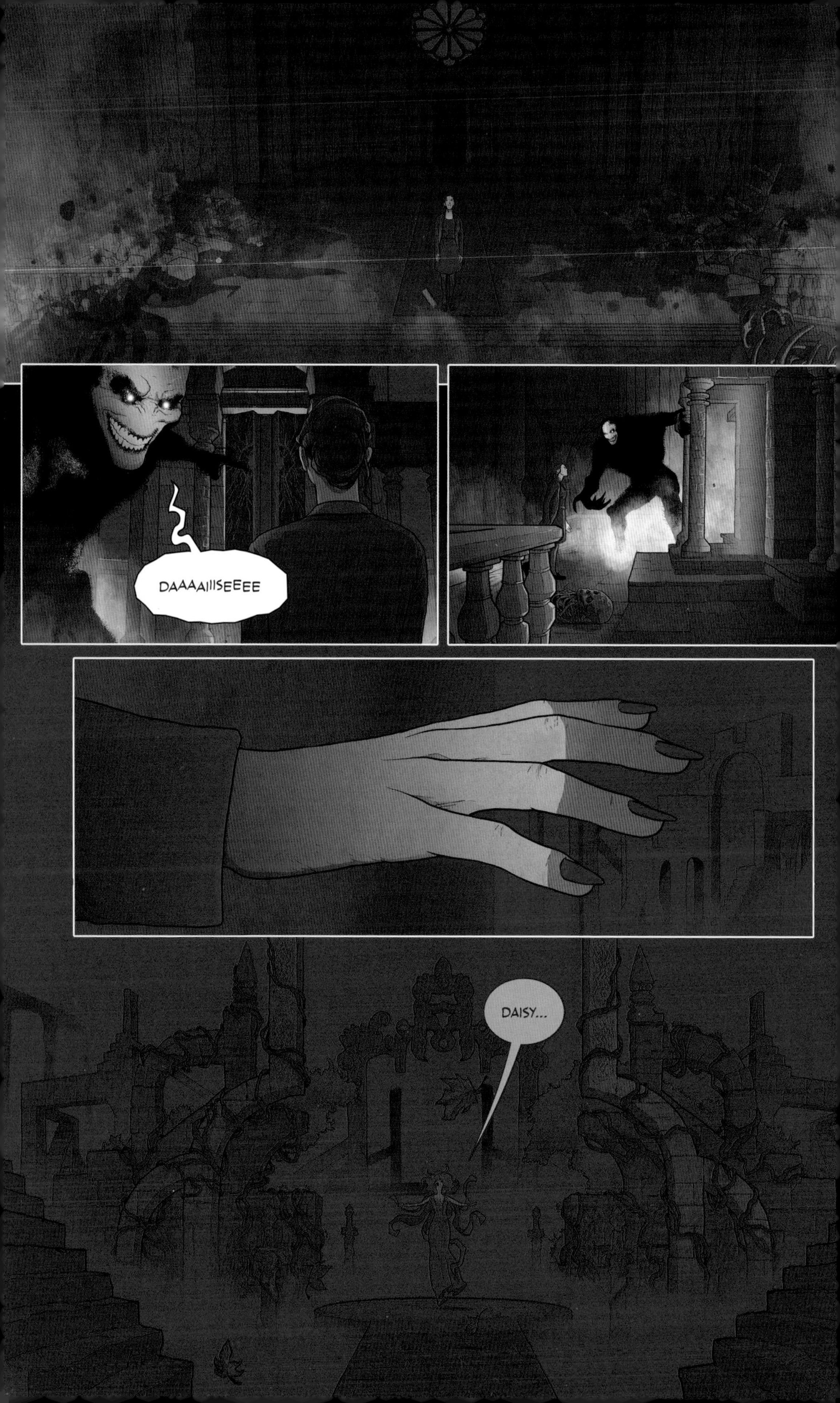
DAAAAIIISEEEE
DAISY...

CHAPTER TWELVE

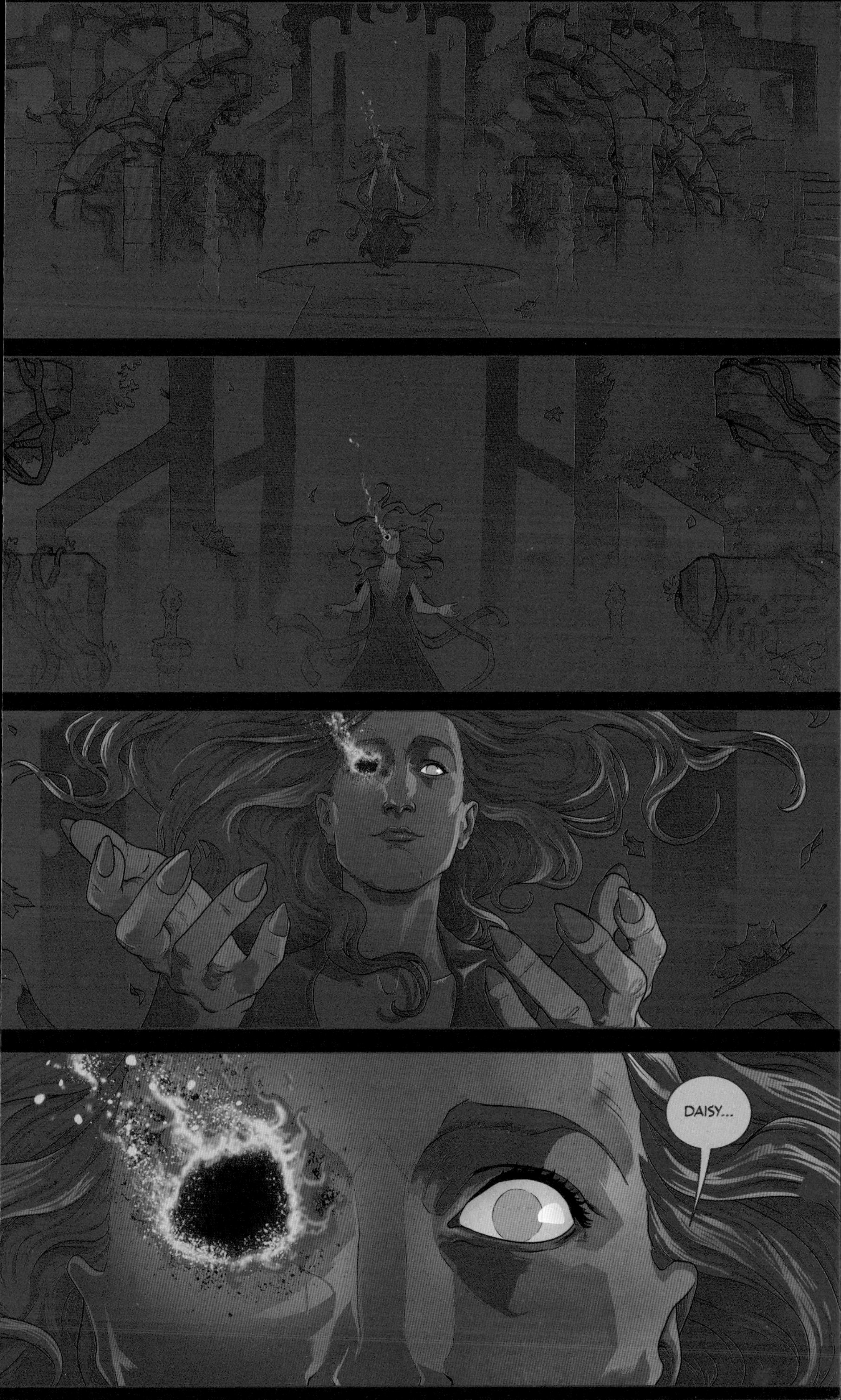
DAISY...

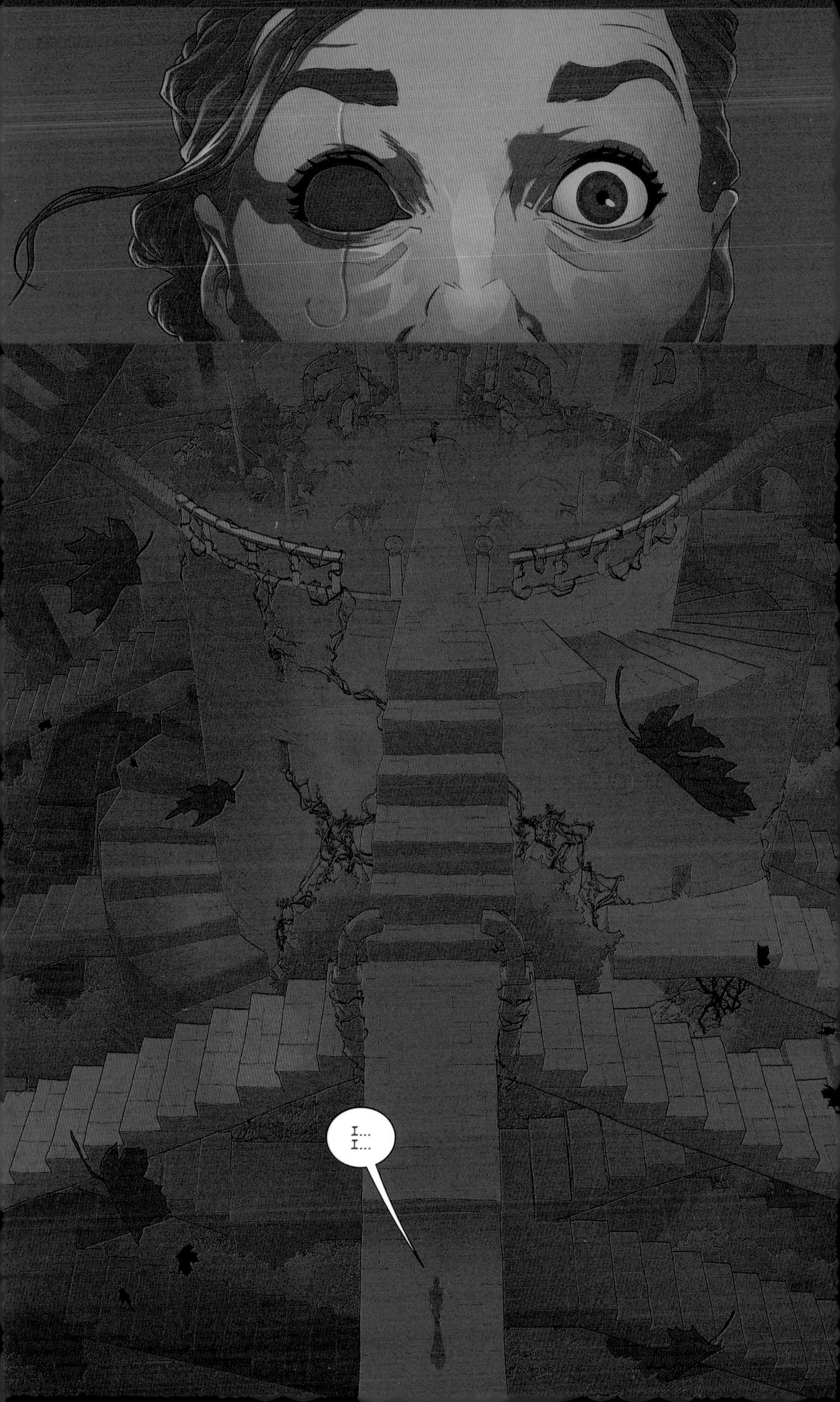
I... I...

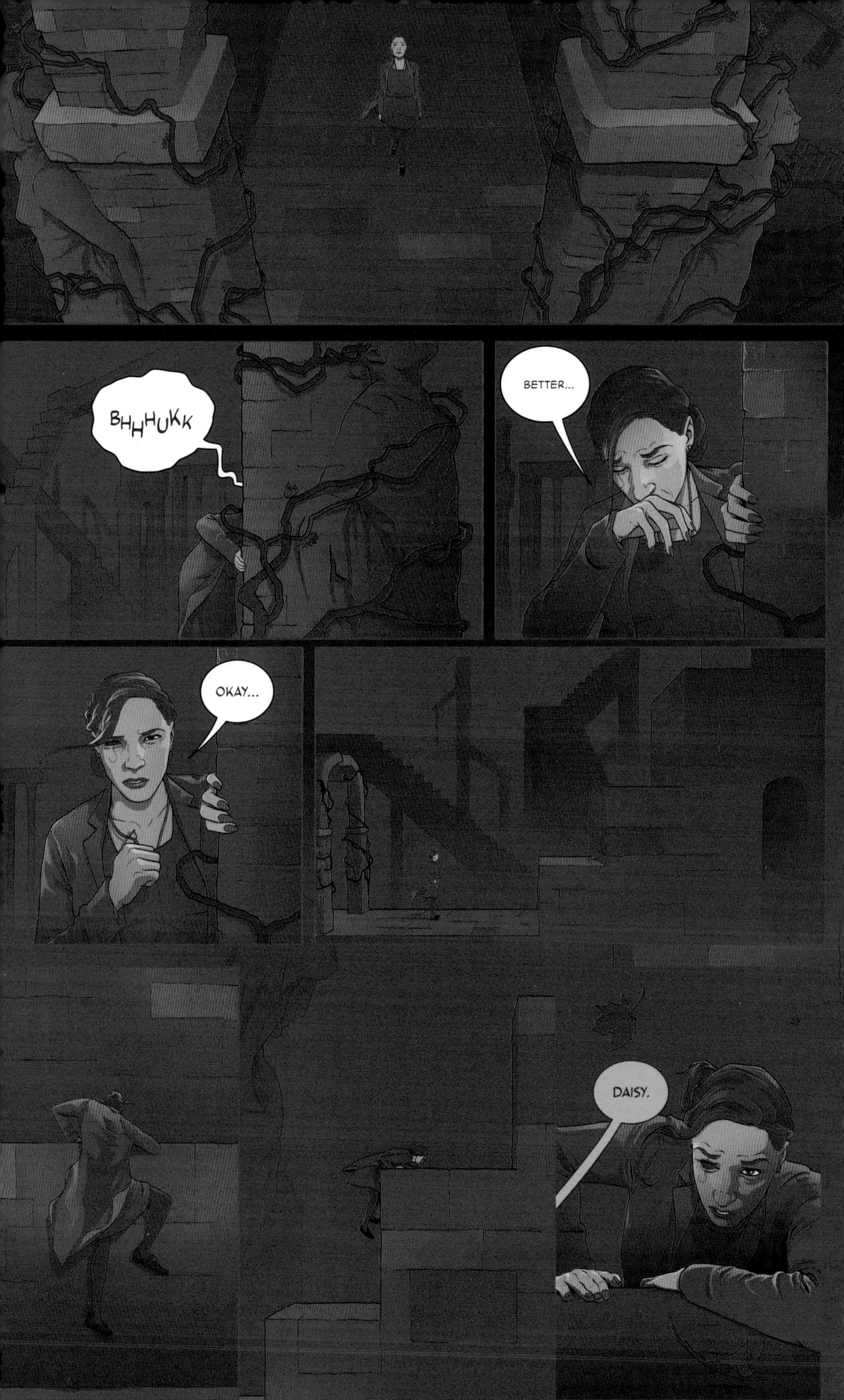
BHHHUKK
BETTER...
OKAY...
DAISY.

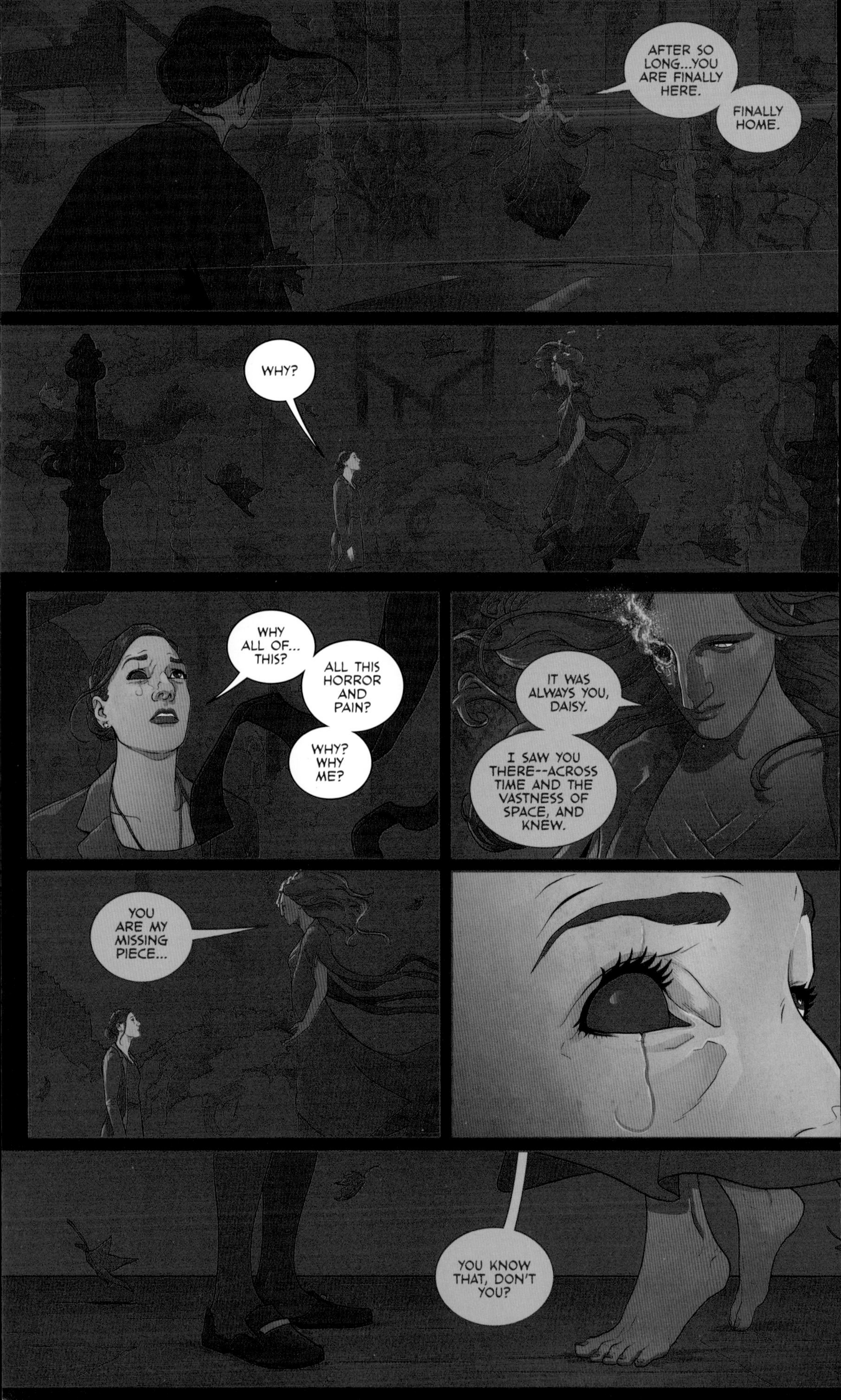

AFTER SO LONG...YOU ARE FINALLY HERE.
FINALLY HOME.
WHY?
WHY ALL OF... THIS?
ALL THIS HORROR AND PAIN?
WHY? WHY ME?
IT WAS ALWAYS YOU, DAISY.
I SAW YOU THERE--ACROSS TIME AND THE VASTNESS OF SPACE, AND KNEW.
YOU ARE MY MISSING PIECE...
YOU KNOW THAT, DON'T YOU?

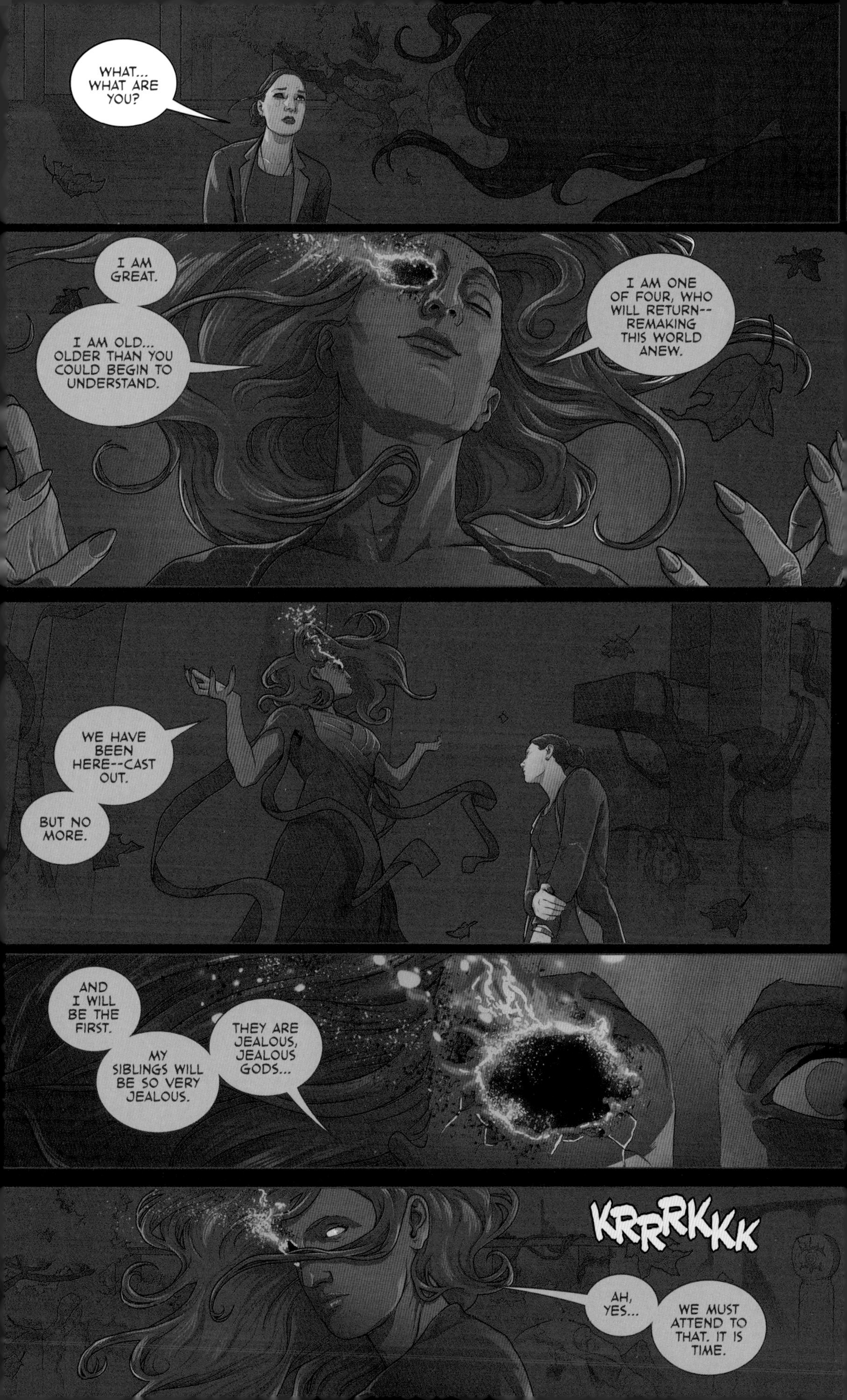
WHAT... WHAT ARE YOU?
I AM GREAT.
I AM OLD... OLDER THAN YOU COULD BEGIN TO UNDERSTAND.
I AM ONE OF FOUR, WHO WILL RETURN-- REMAKING THIS WORLD ANEW.
WE HAVE BEEN HERE--CAST OUT.
BUT NO MORE.
AND I WILL BE THE FIRST.
MY SIBLINGS WILL BE SO VERY JEALOUS.
THEY ARE JEALOUS, JEALOUS GODS...
KRRRKKK
AH, YES...
WE MUST ATTEND TO THAT. IT IS TIME.

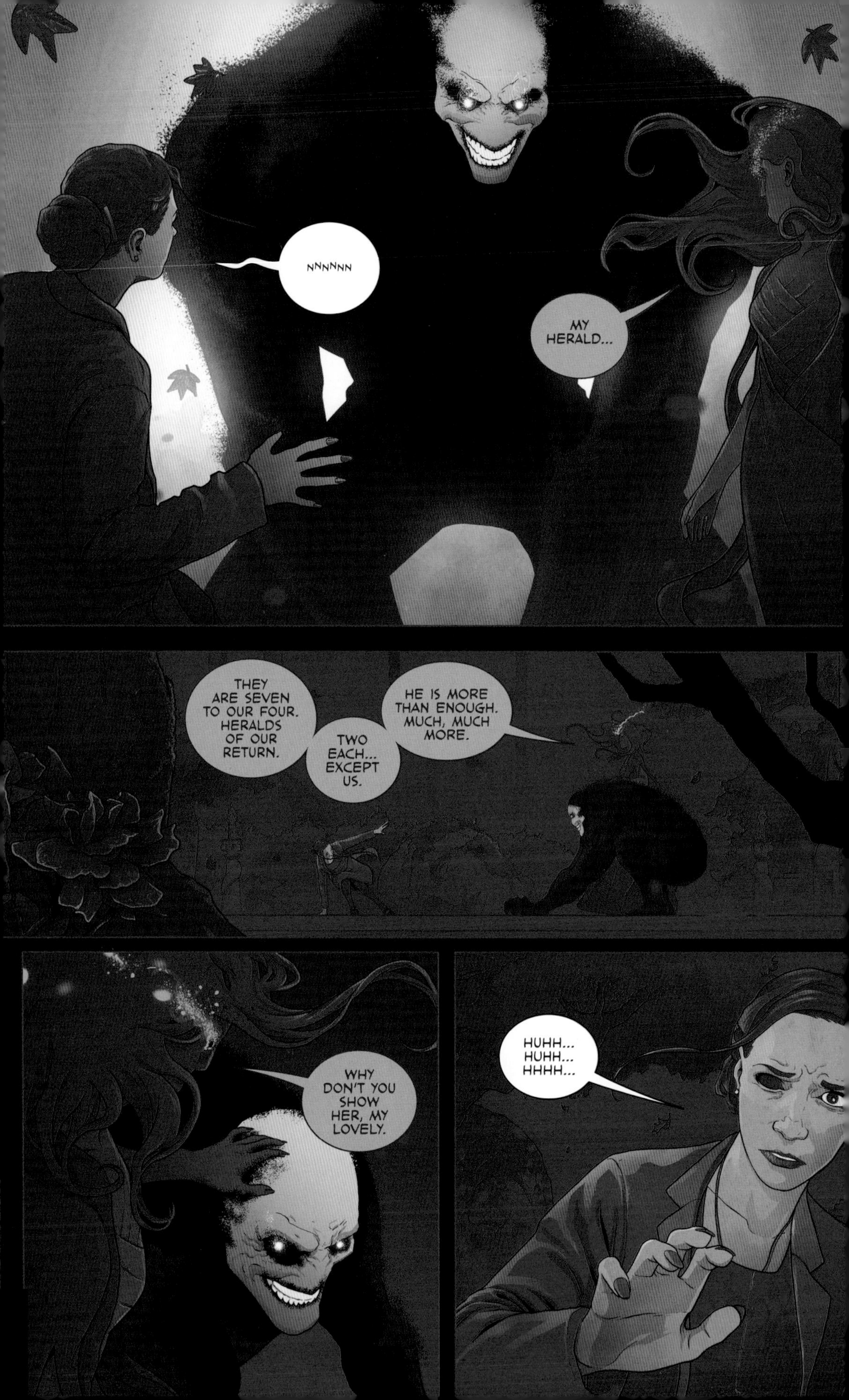
NNNNNN
MY HERALD...
THEY ARE SEVEN TO OUR FOUR. HERALDS OF OUR RETURN.
TWO EACH... EXCEPT US.
HE IS MORE THAN ENOUGH. MUCH, MUCH MORE.
WHY DON'T YOU SHOW HER, MY LOVELY.
HUHH... HUHH... HHHH...

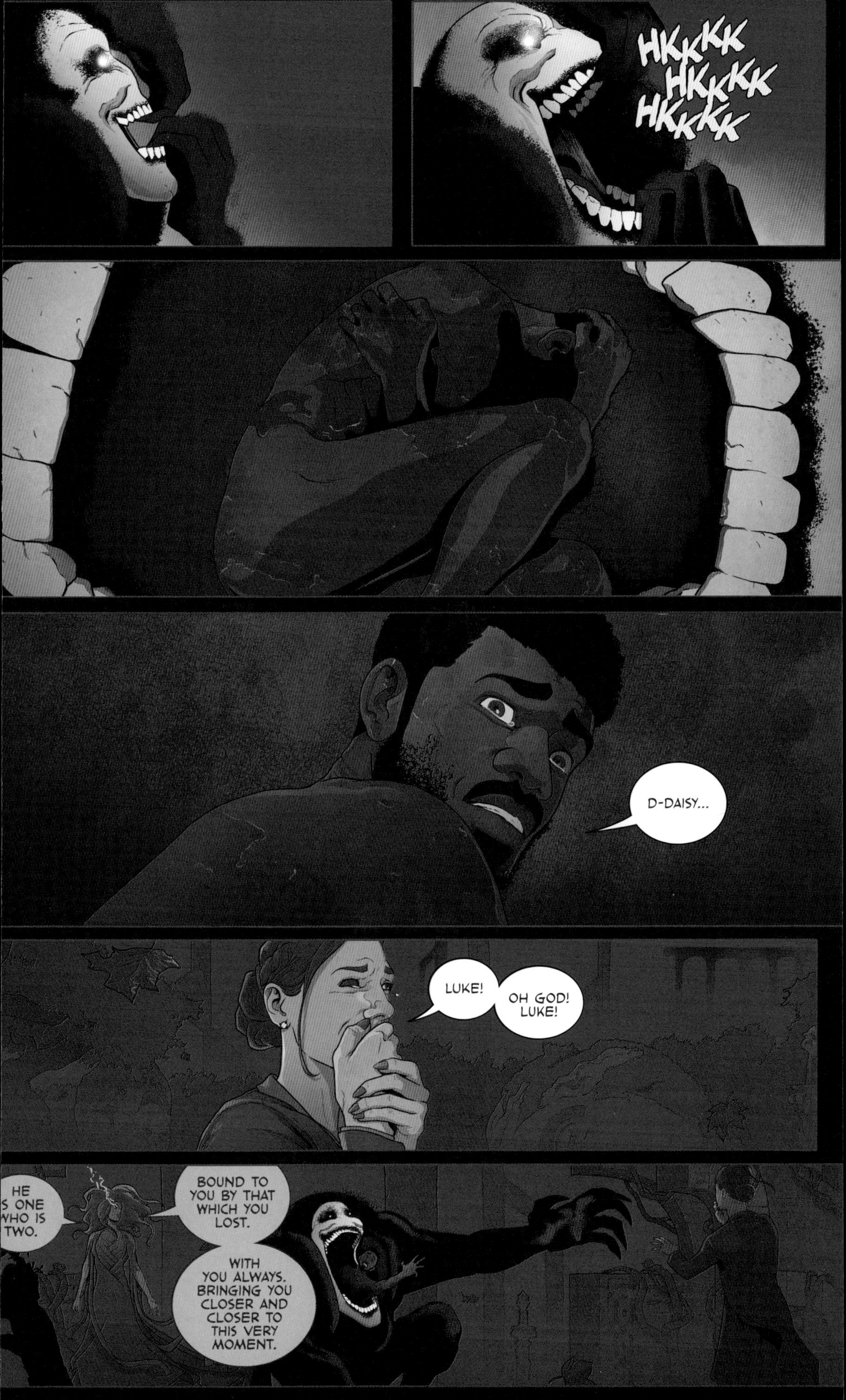
HKKKK
HKKKK
HKKKK
D-DAISY...
LUKE!
OH GOD! LUKE!
HE S ONE WHO IS TWO.
BOUND TO YOU BY THAT WHICH YOU LOST.
WITH YOU ALWAYS. BRINGING YOU CLOSER AND CLOSER TO THIS VERY MOMENT.

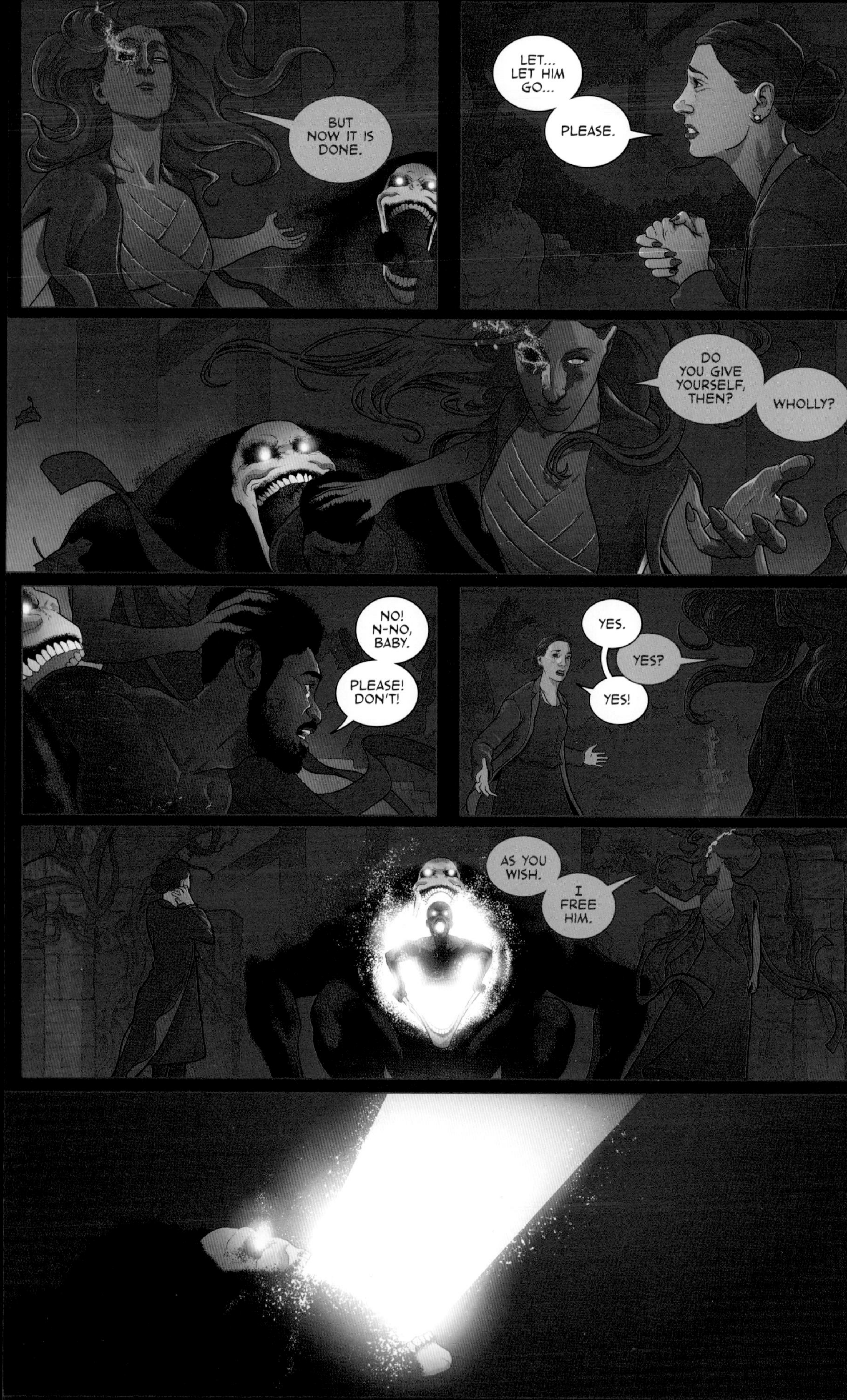
BUT NOW IT IS DONE.
LET... LET HIM GO...
PLEASE.
DO YOU GIVE YOURSELF, THEN?
WHOLLY?
NO! N-NO, BABY.
PLEASE! DON'T!
YES.
YES?
YES!
AS YOU WISH.
I FREE HIM.

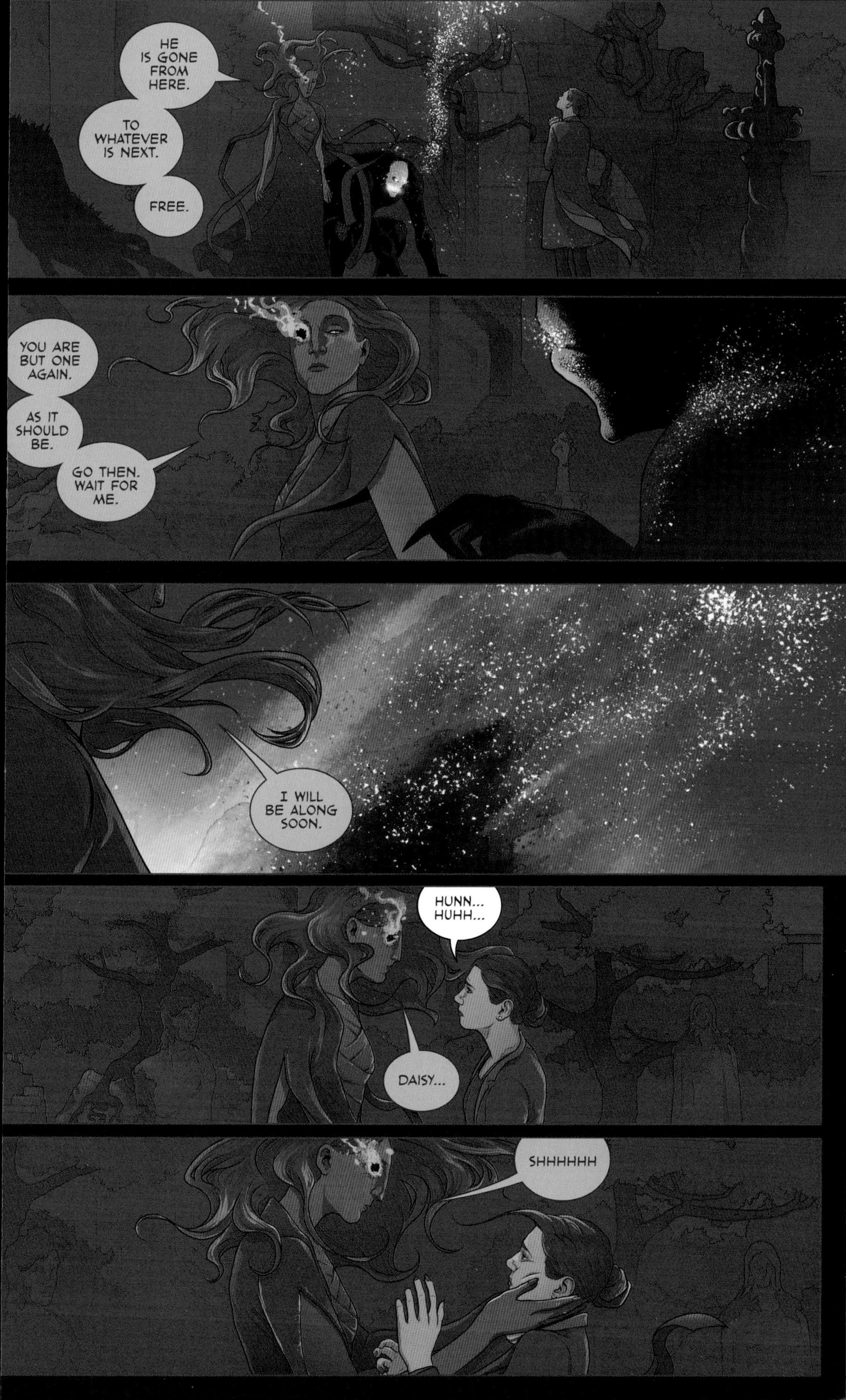
HE IS GONE FROM HERE.
TO WHATEVER IS NEXT.
FREE.
YOU ARE BUT ONE AGAIN.
AS IT SHOULD BE.
GO THEN. WAIT FOR ME.
I WILL BE ALONG SOON.
HUNN... HUHH...
DAISY...
SHHHHHH

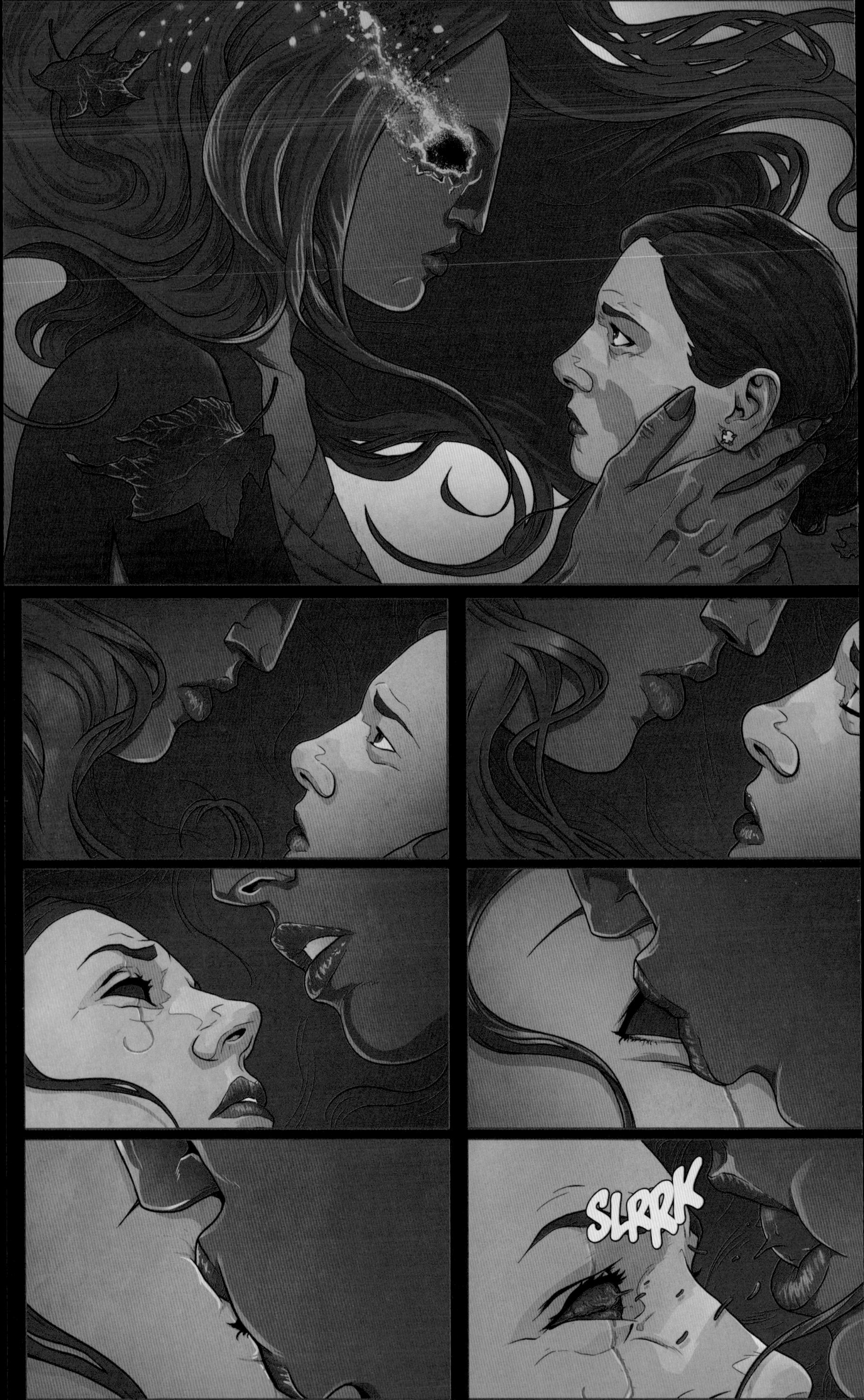
SLRRK

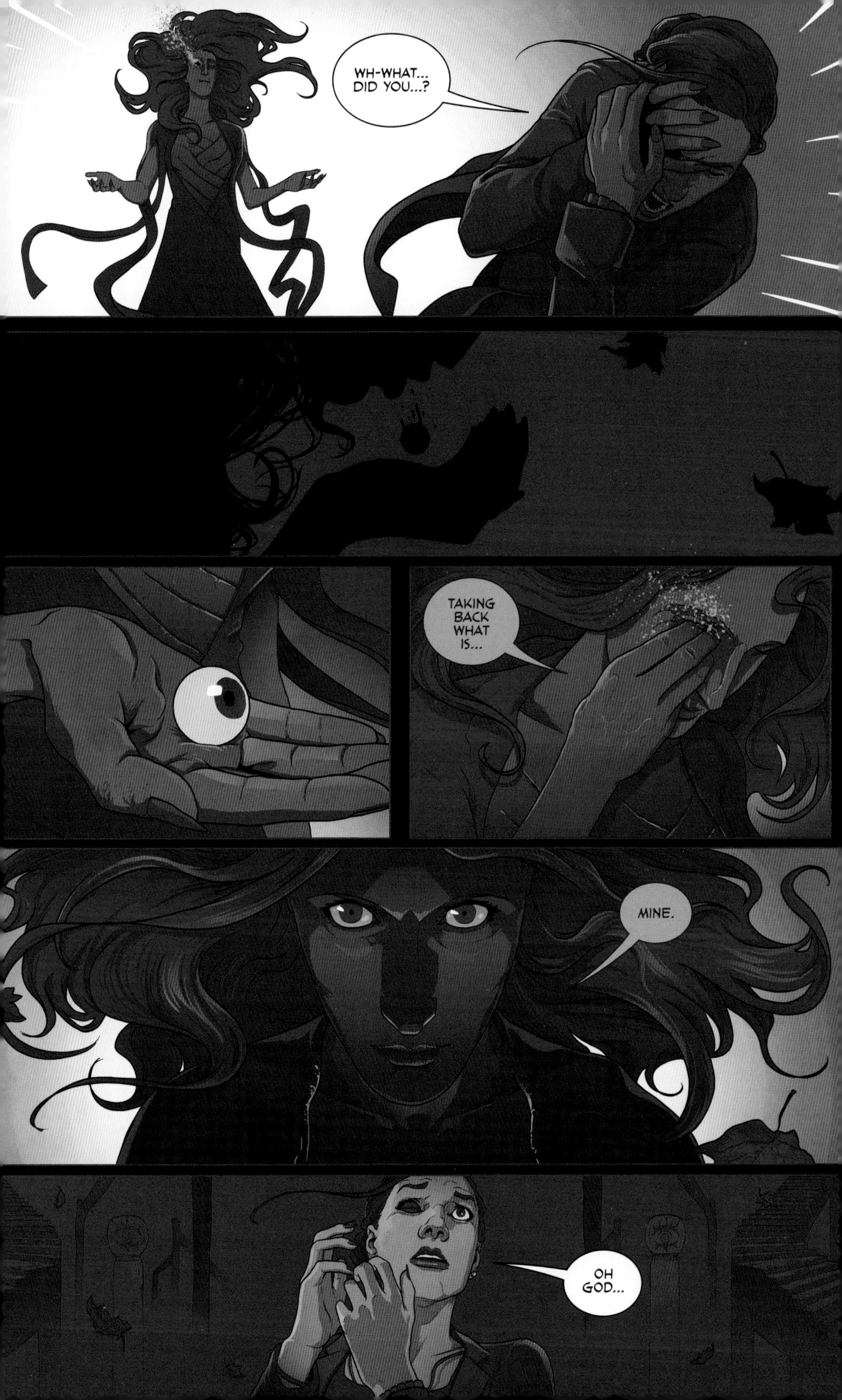

WH-WHAT... DID YOU...?
TAKING BACK WHAT IS...
MINE.
OH GOD...

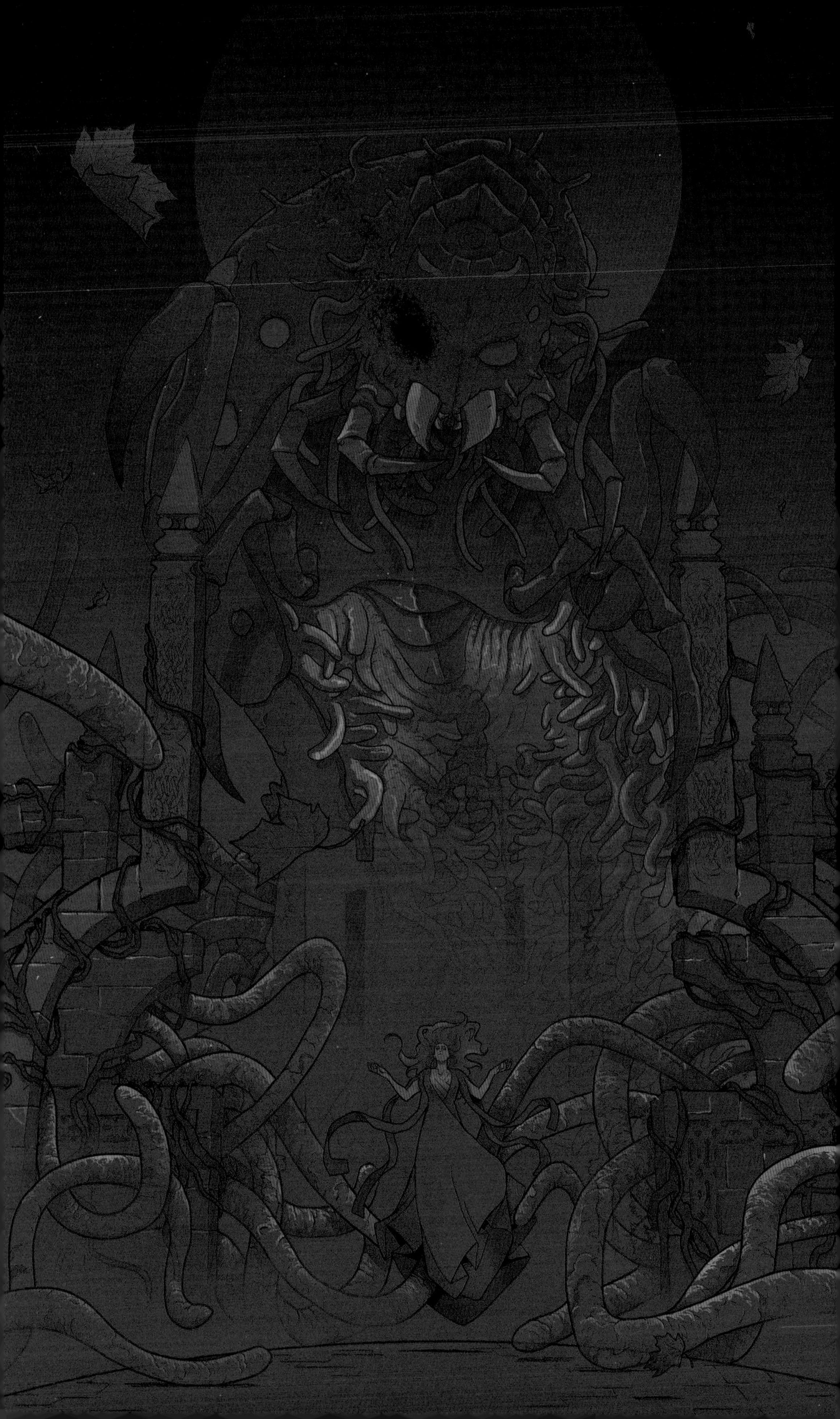

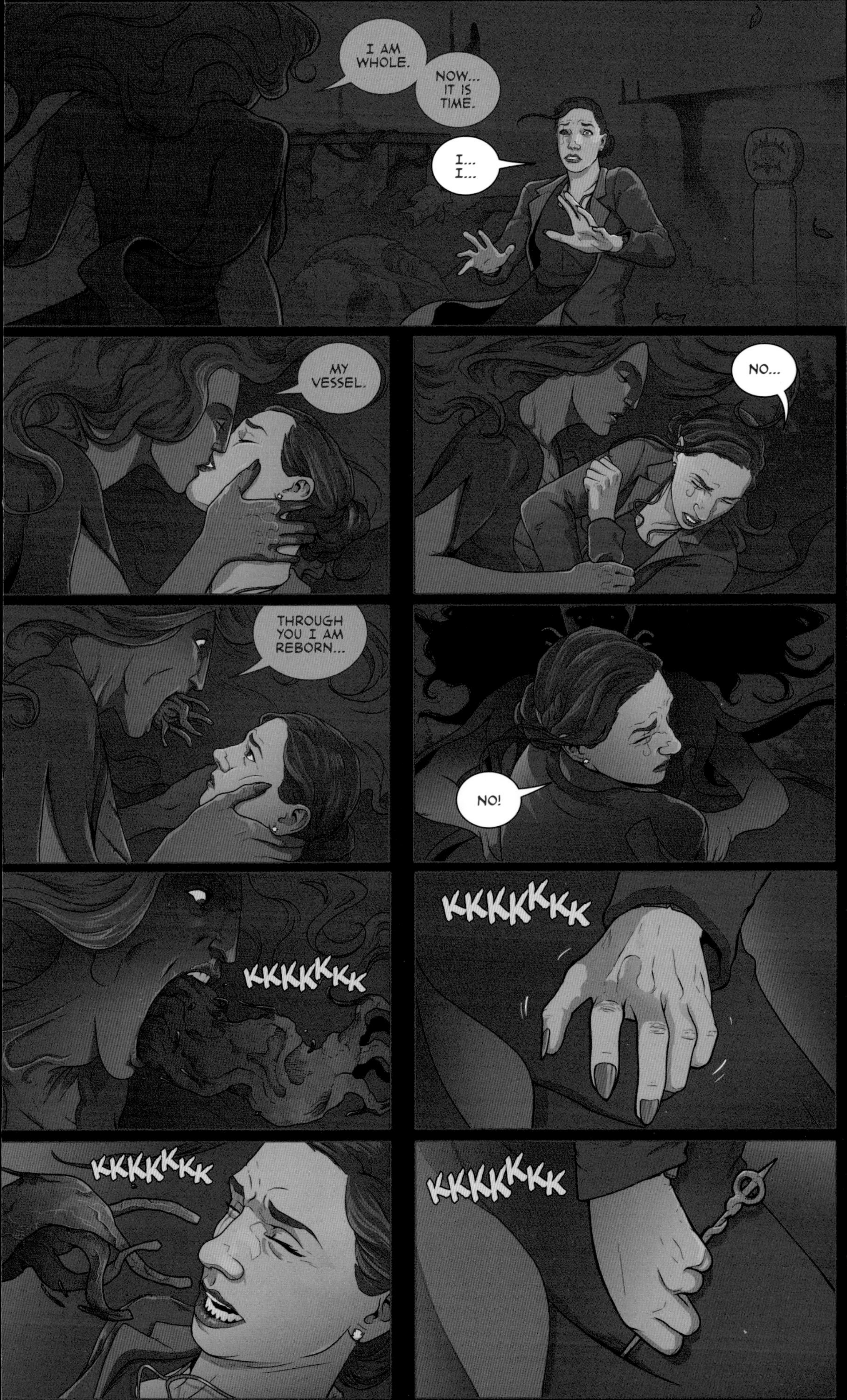
I AM WHOLE.
NOW... IT IS TIME.
I... I...
MY VESSEL.
NO...
THROUGH YOU I AM REBORN...
NO!
KKKKKKK
KKKKKKK
KKKKKKK
KKKKKKK

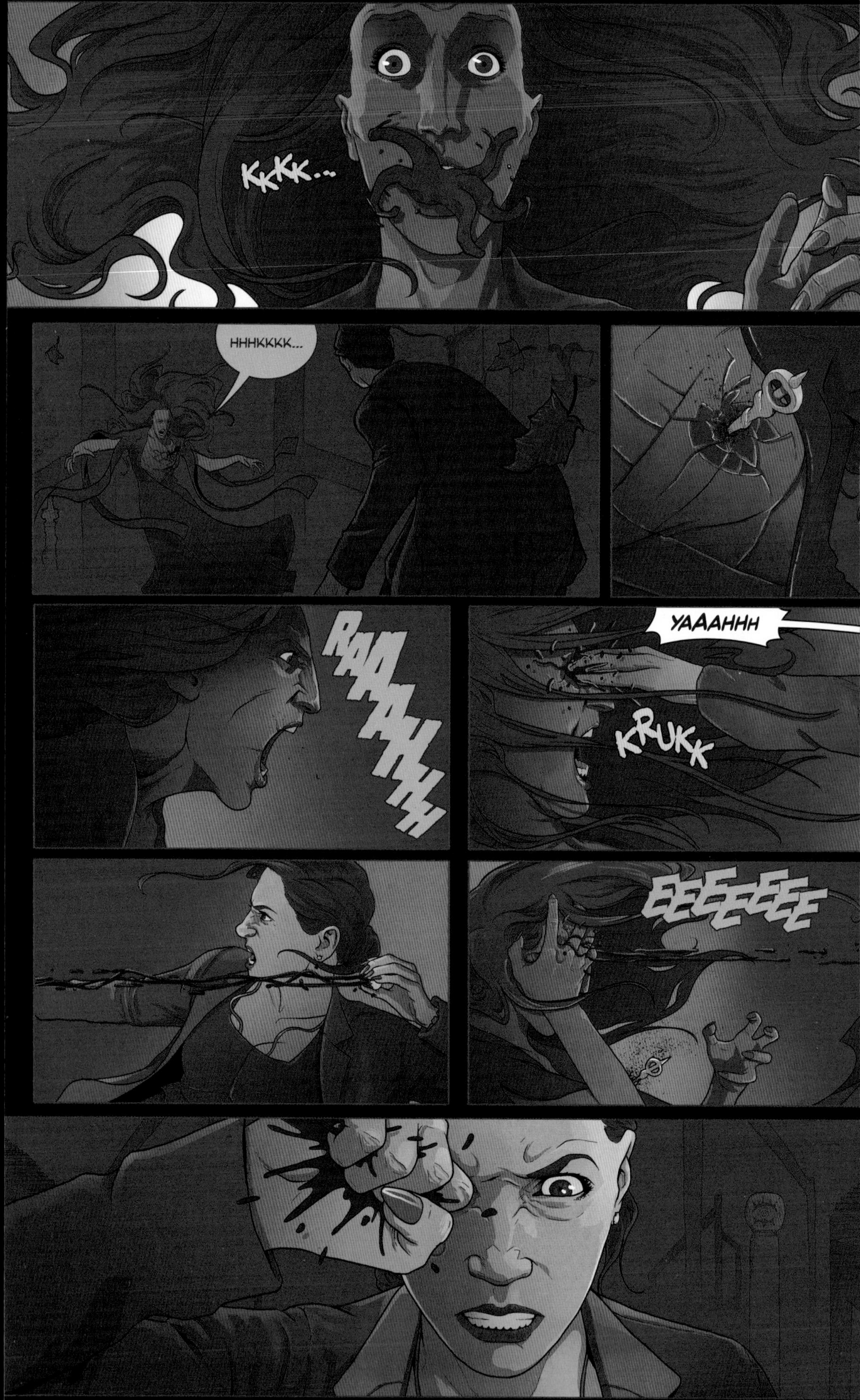
KKKK...
HHHKKKK...
RAAAAHHHH
YAAAHHH
KRUKK
EEEEEEEE

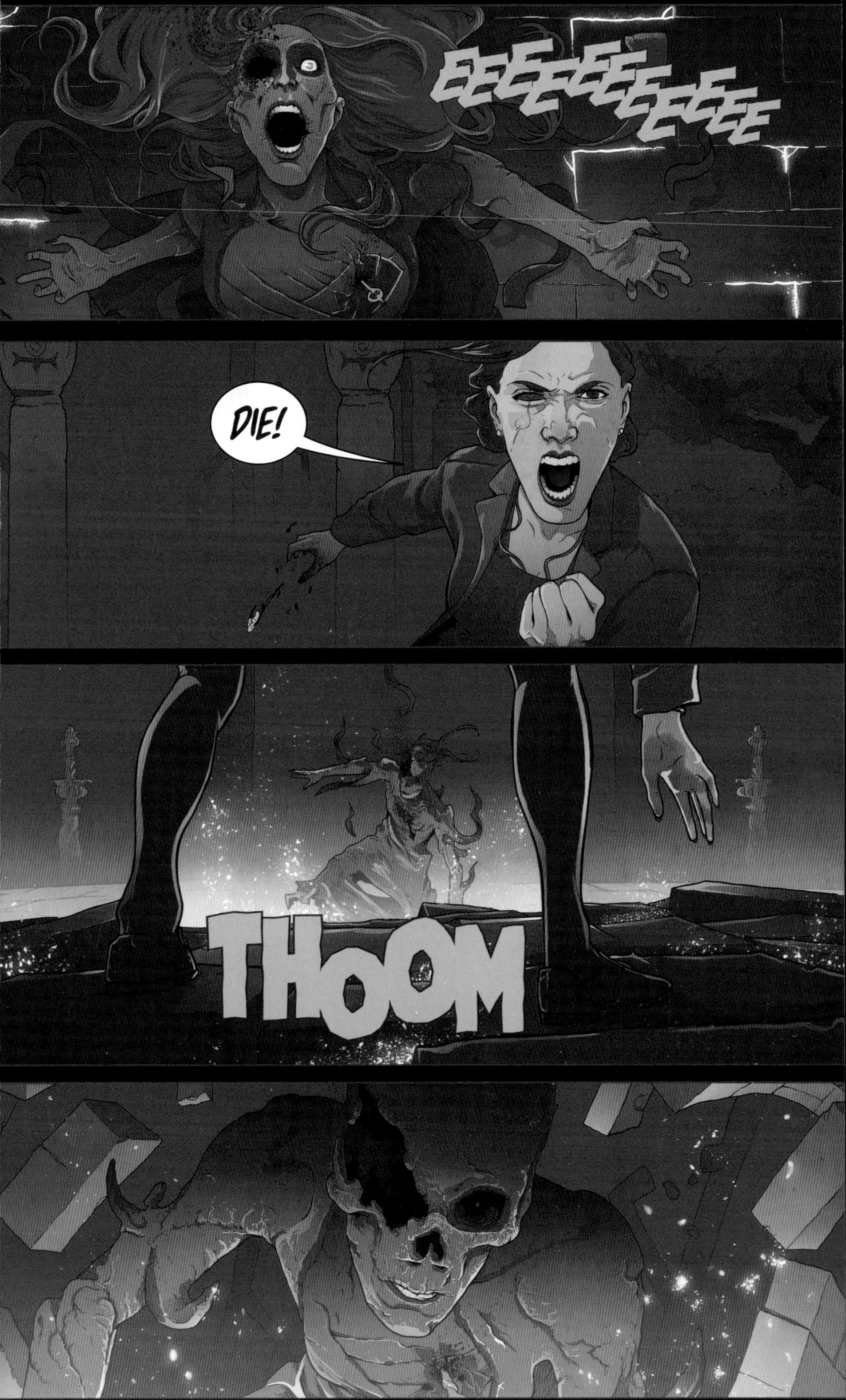
EEEEEEEEEEEEE
DIE!
THOOM

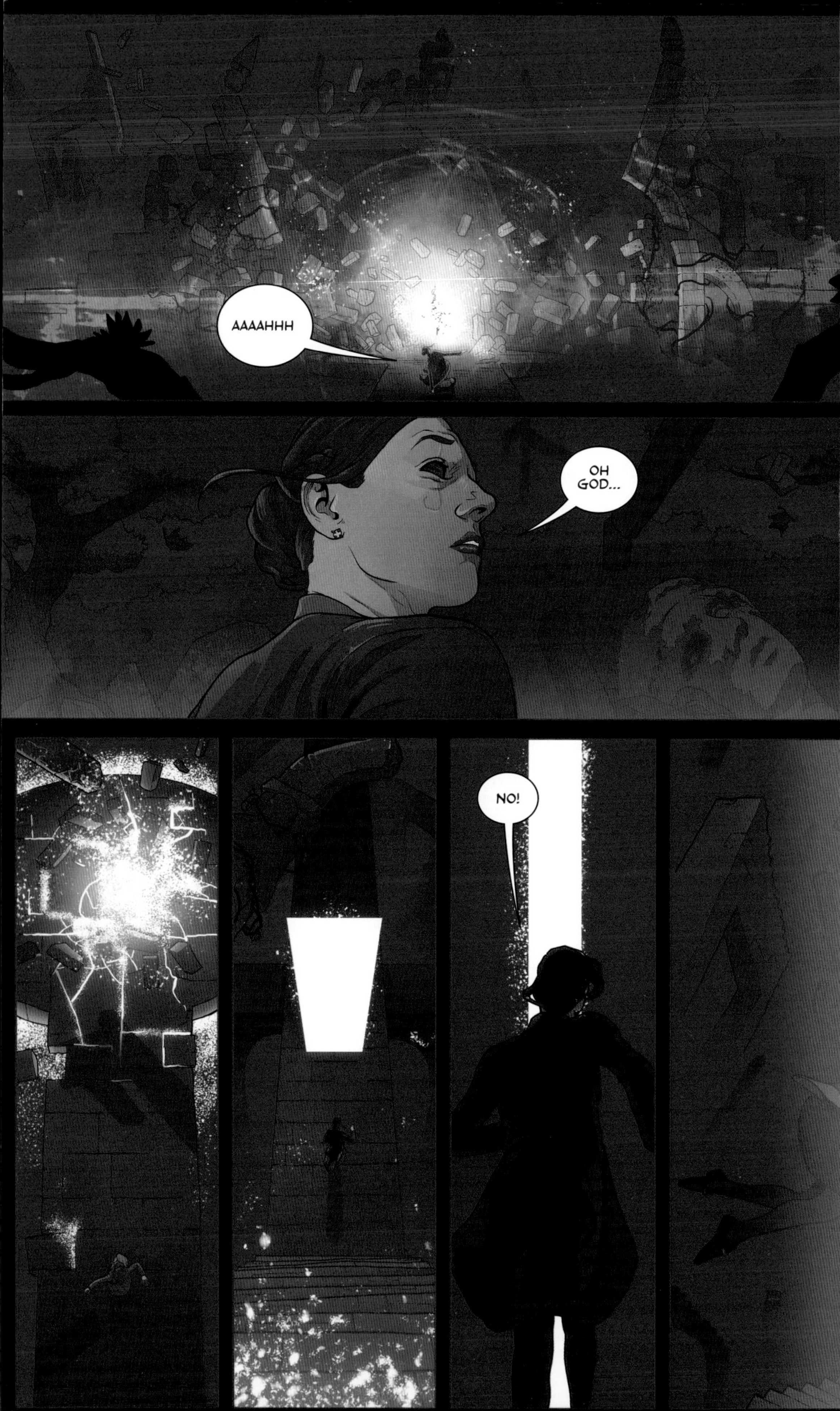
AAAAHHH
OH GOD...
NO!

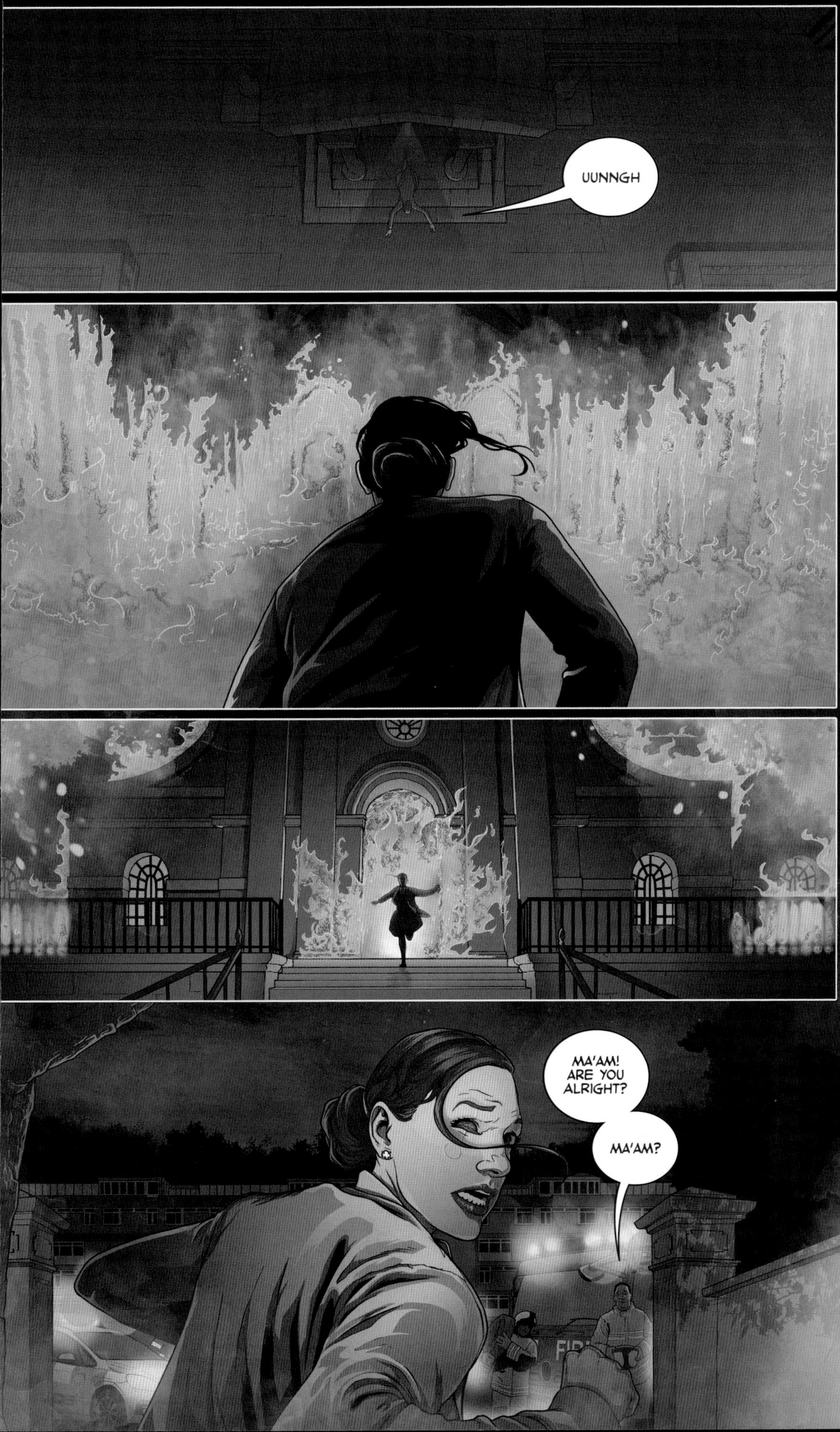
UUNNGH
MA'AM! ARE YOU ALRIGHT?
MA'AM?

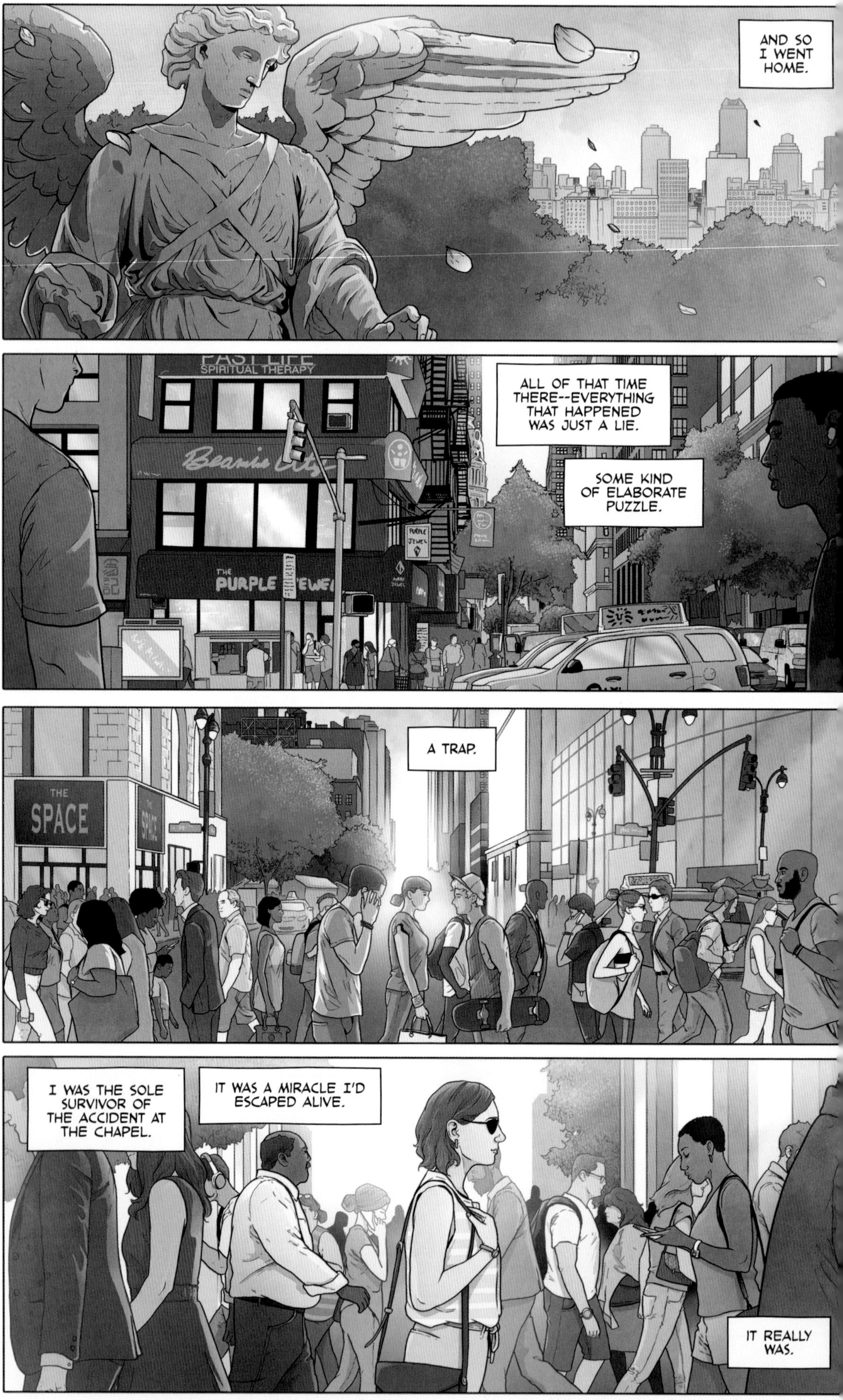
AND SO I WENT HOME.
PAST LIFE
SPIRITUAL THERAPY
ALL OF THAT TIME THERE--EVERYTHING THAT HAPPENED WAS JUST A LIE.
SOME KIND OF ELABORATE PUZZLE.
THE SPACE
A TRAP.
I WAS THE SOLE SURVIVOR OF THE ACCIDENT AT THE CHAPEL.
IT WAS A MIRACLE I'D ESCAPED ALIVE.
IT REALLY WAS.

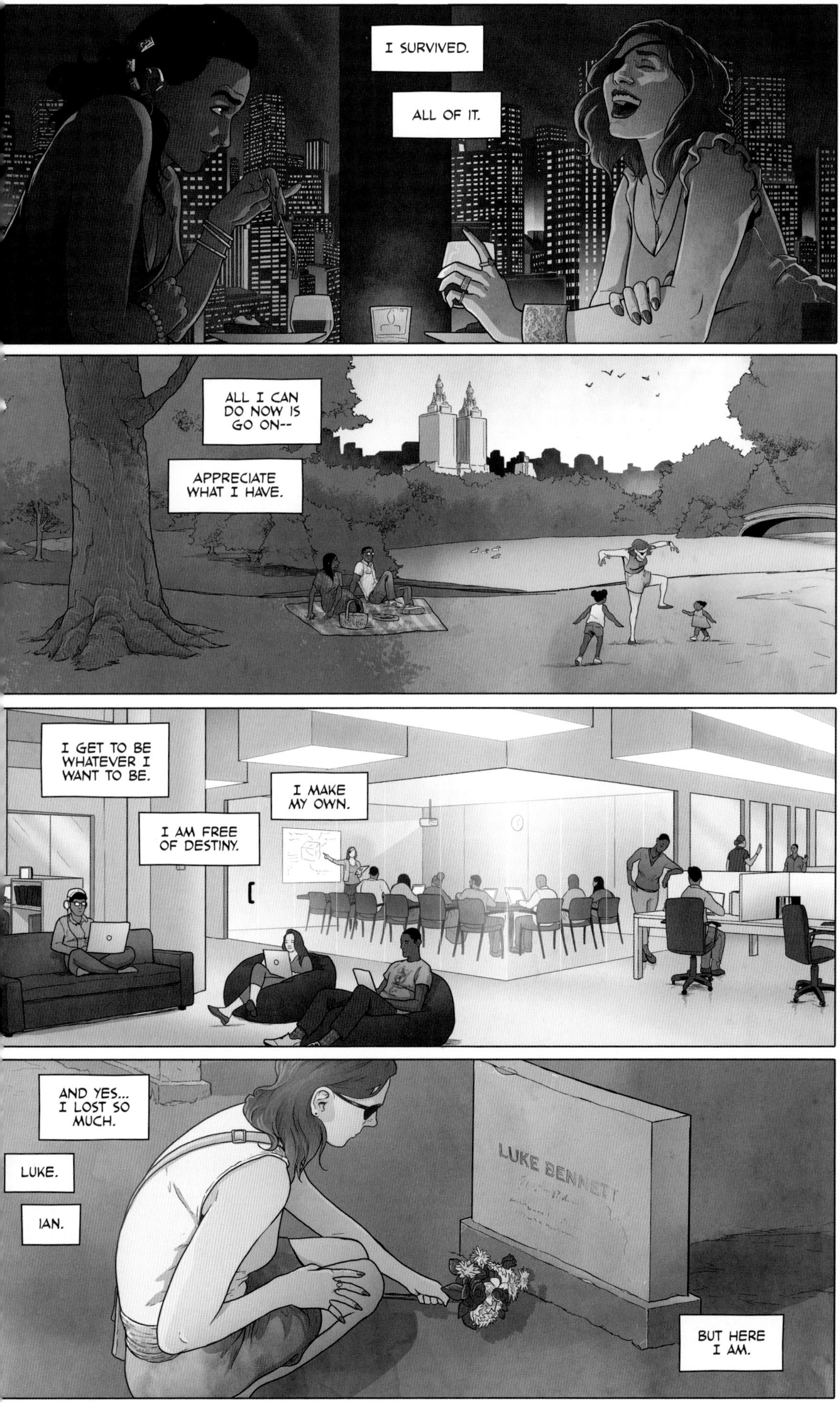
I SURVIVED.
ALL OF IT.
ALL I CAN DO NOW IS GO ON--
APPRECIATE WHAT I HAVE.
I GET TO BE WHATEVER I WANT TO BE.
I AM FREE OF DESTINY.
I MAKE MY OWN.
AND YES... I LOST SO MUCH.
LUKE.
IAN.
LUKE BENNETT
BUT HERE I AM.

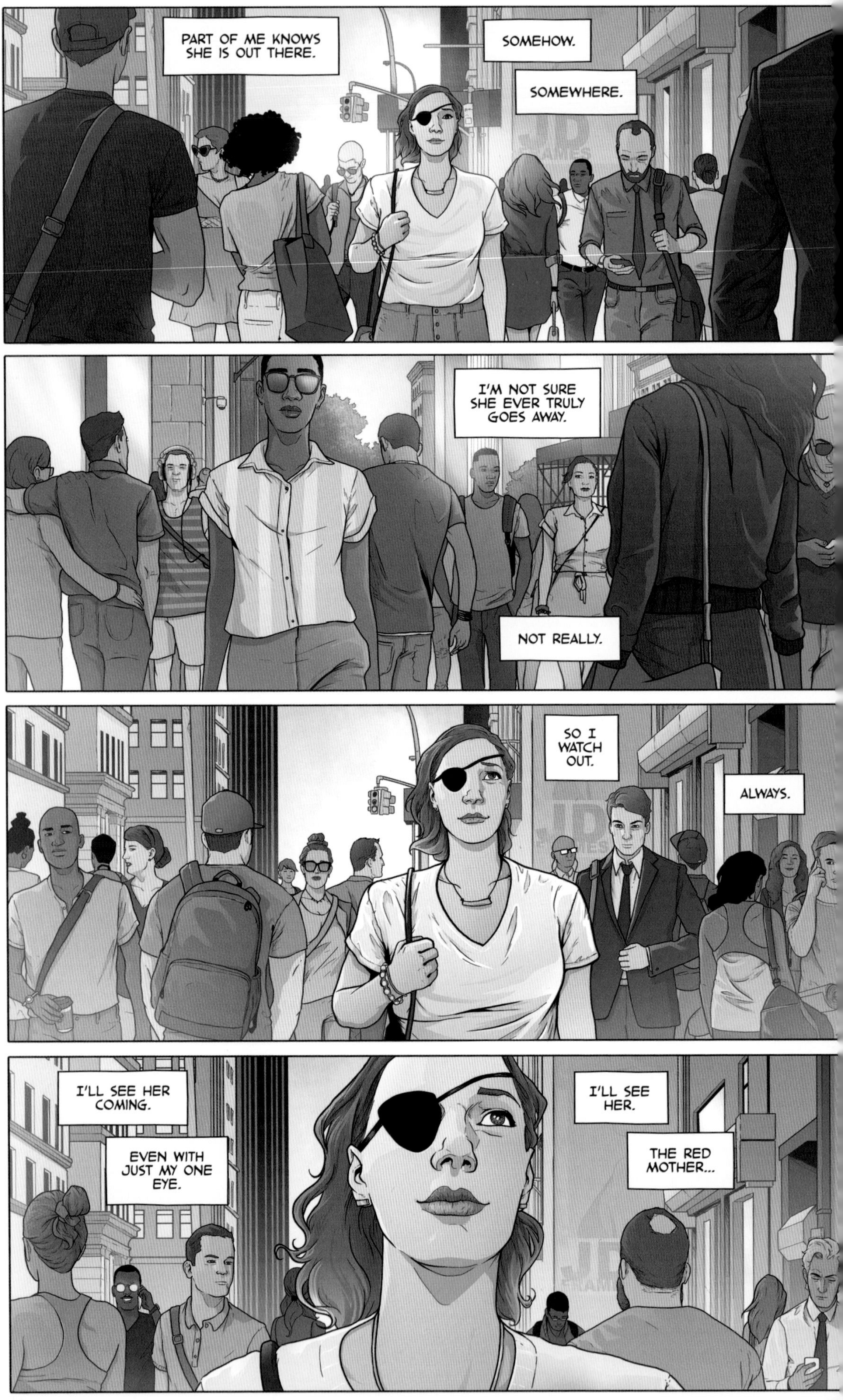
PART OF ME KNOWS SHE IS OUT THERE.
SOMEHOW.
SOMEWHERE.
I'M NOT SURE SHE EVER TRULY GOES AWAY.
NOT REALLY.
SO I WATCH OUT.
ALWAYS.
I'LL SEE HER COMING.
EVEN WITH JUST MY ONE EYE.
I'LL SEE HER.
THE RED MOTHER...

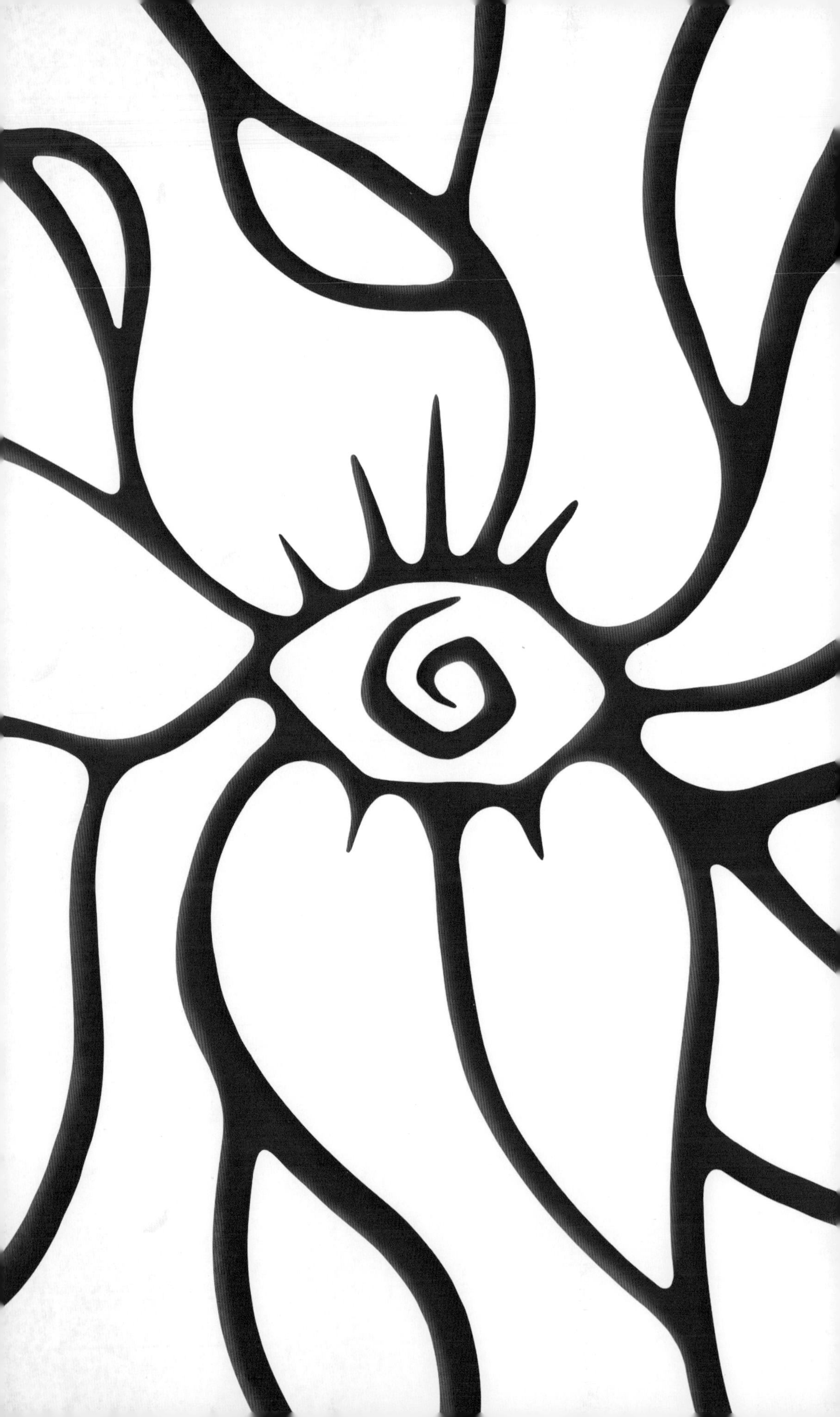

COVER
GALLERY

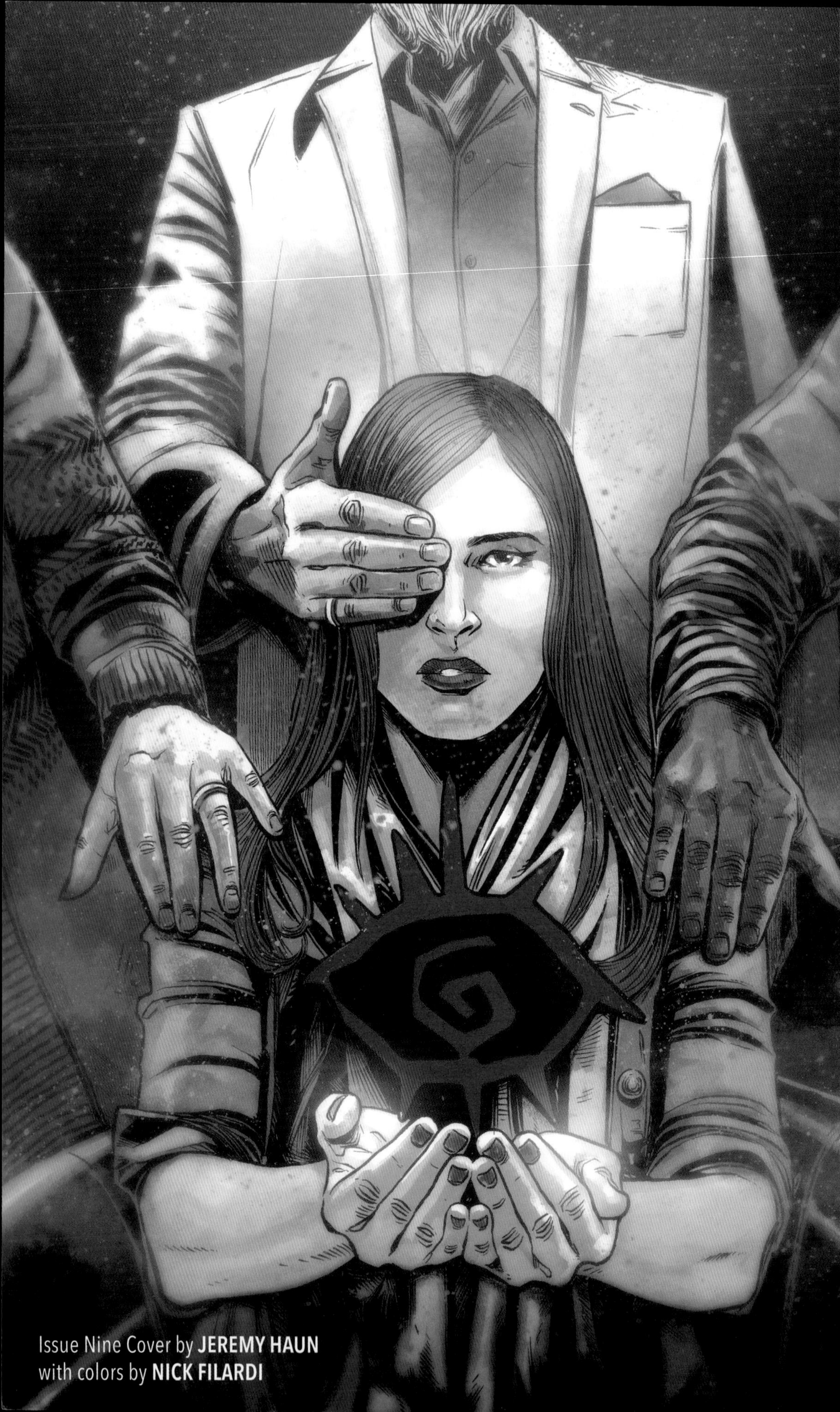

Issue Nine Cover by **JEREMY HAUN**
with colors by **NICK FILARDI**

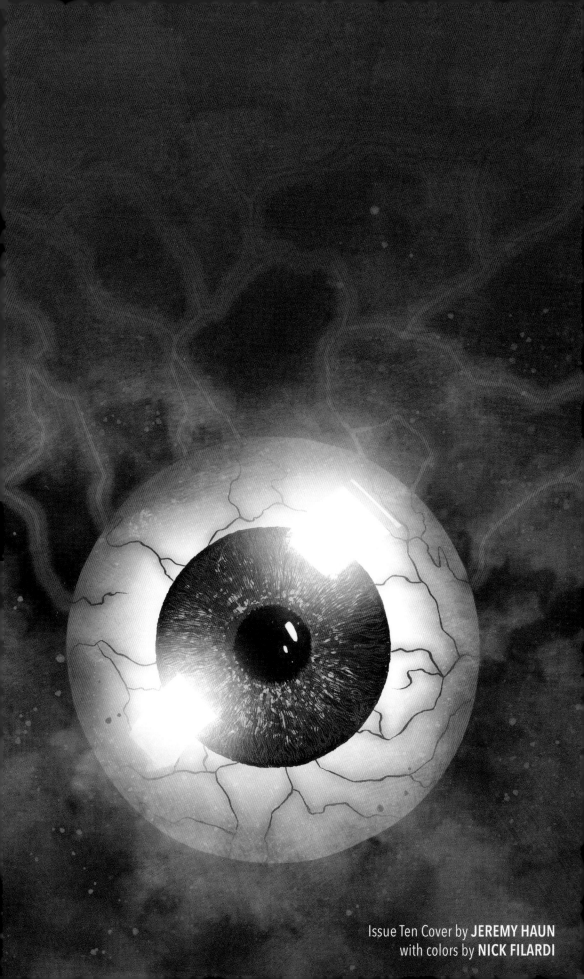

Issue Ten Cover by **JEREMY HAUN**
with colors by **NICK FILARDI**

Issue Eleven Cover by **JEREMY HAUN**
with colors by **NICK FILARDI**

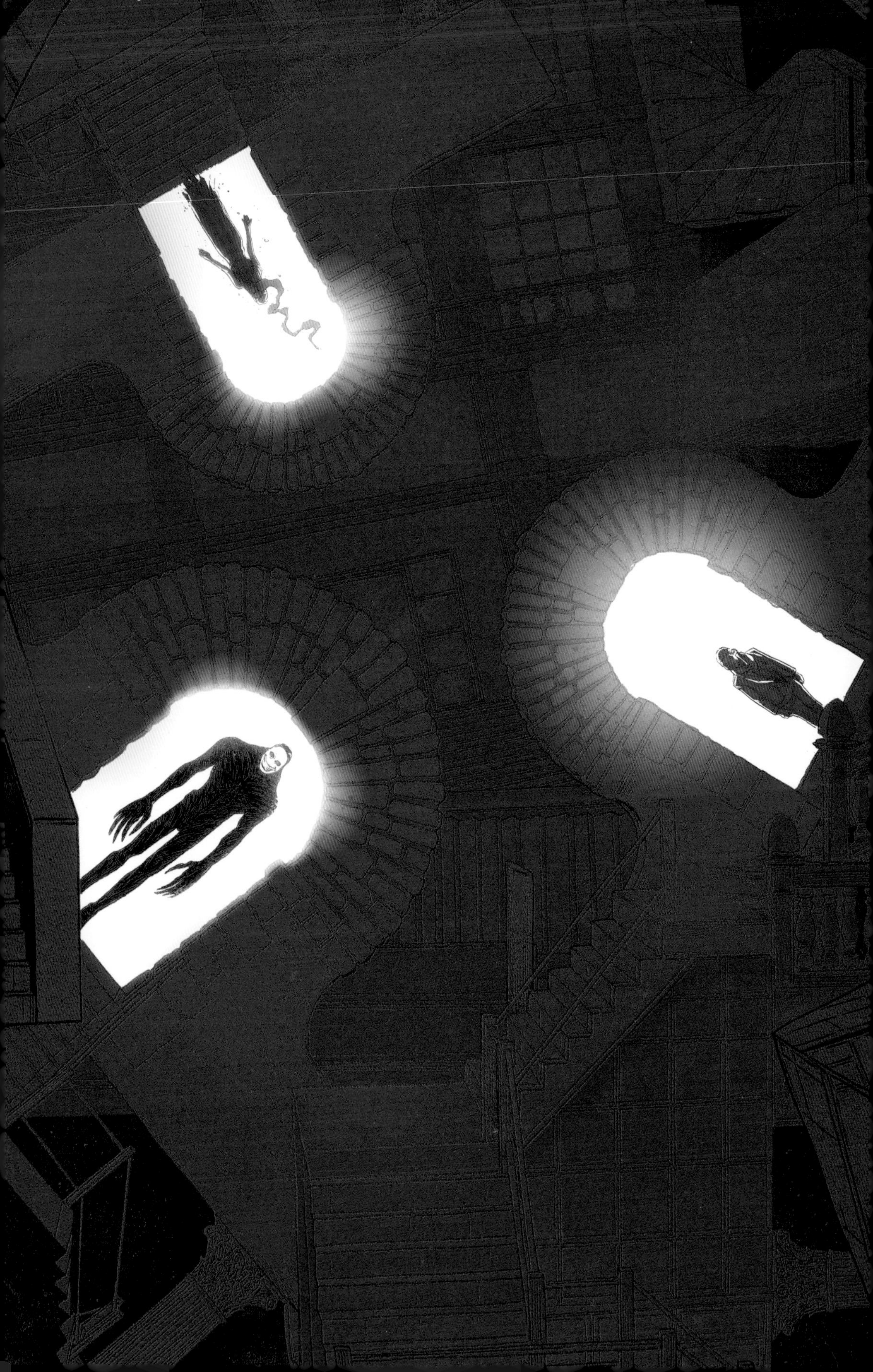

Issue Twelve Cover by **JEREMY HAUN**
with colors by **NICK FILARDI**

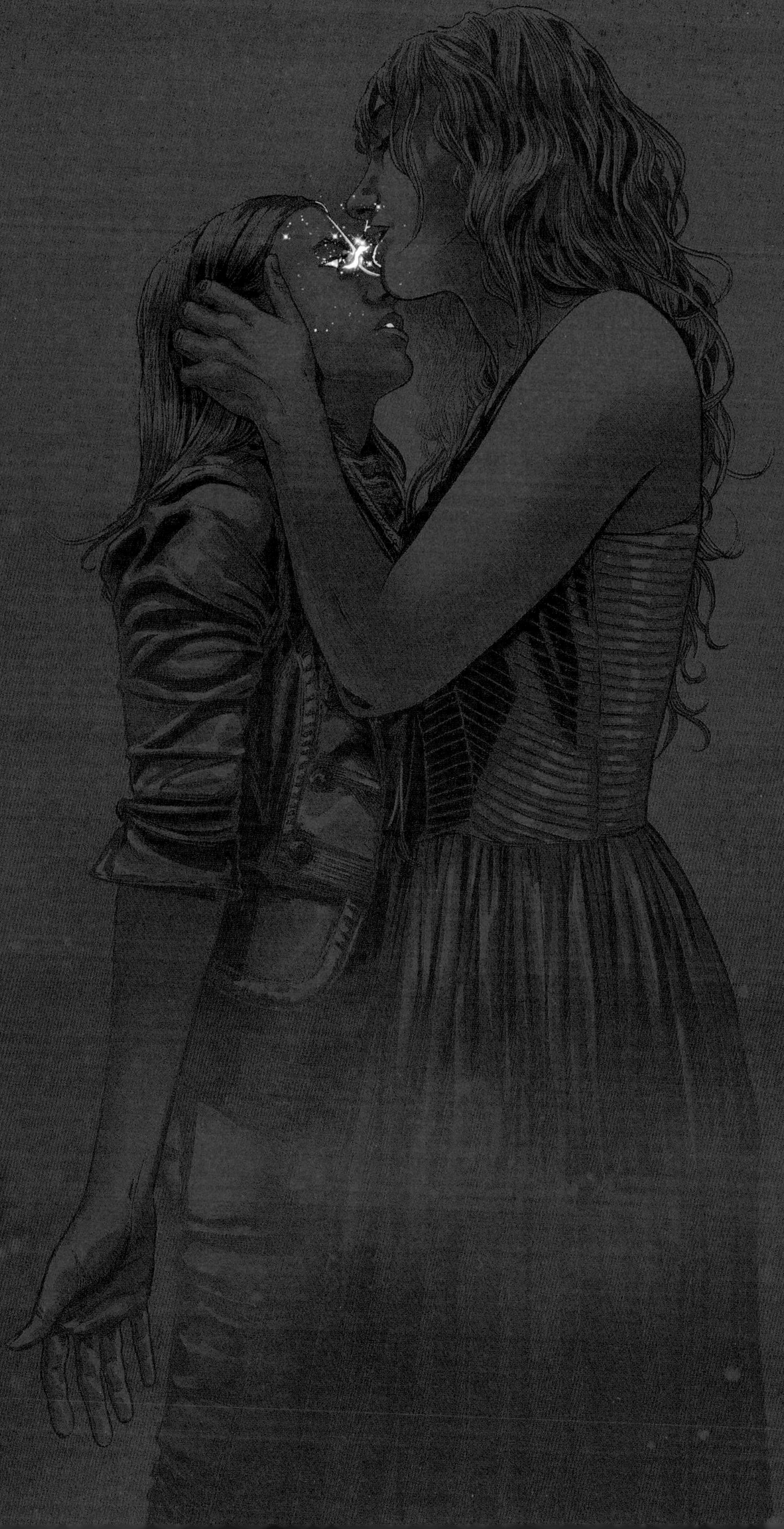

ADDITIONAL ARTWORK BY

DANNY LUCKERT

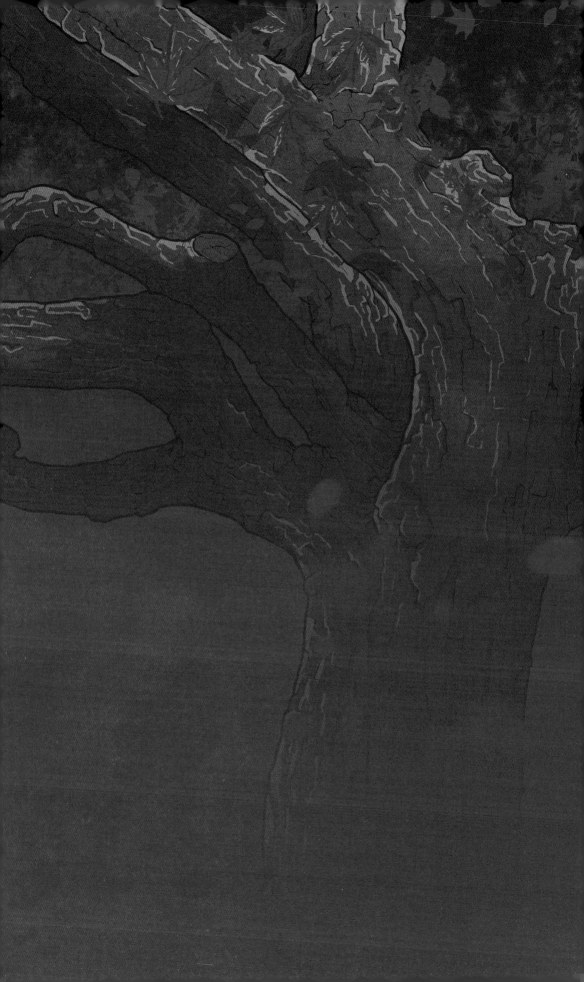

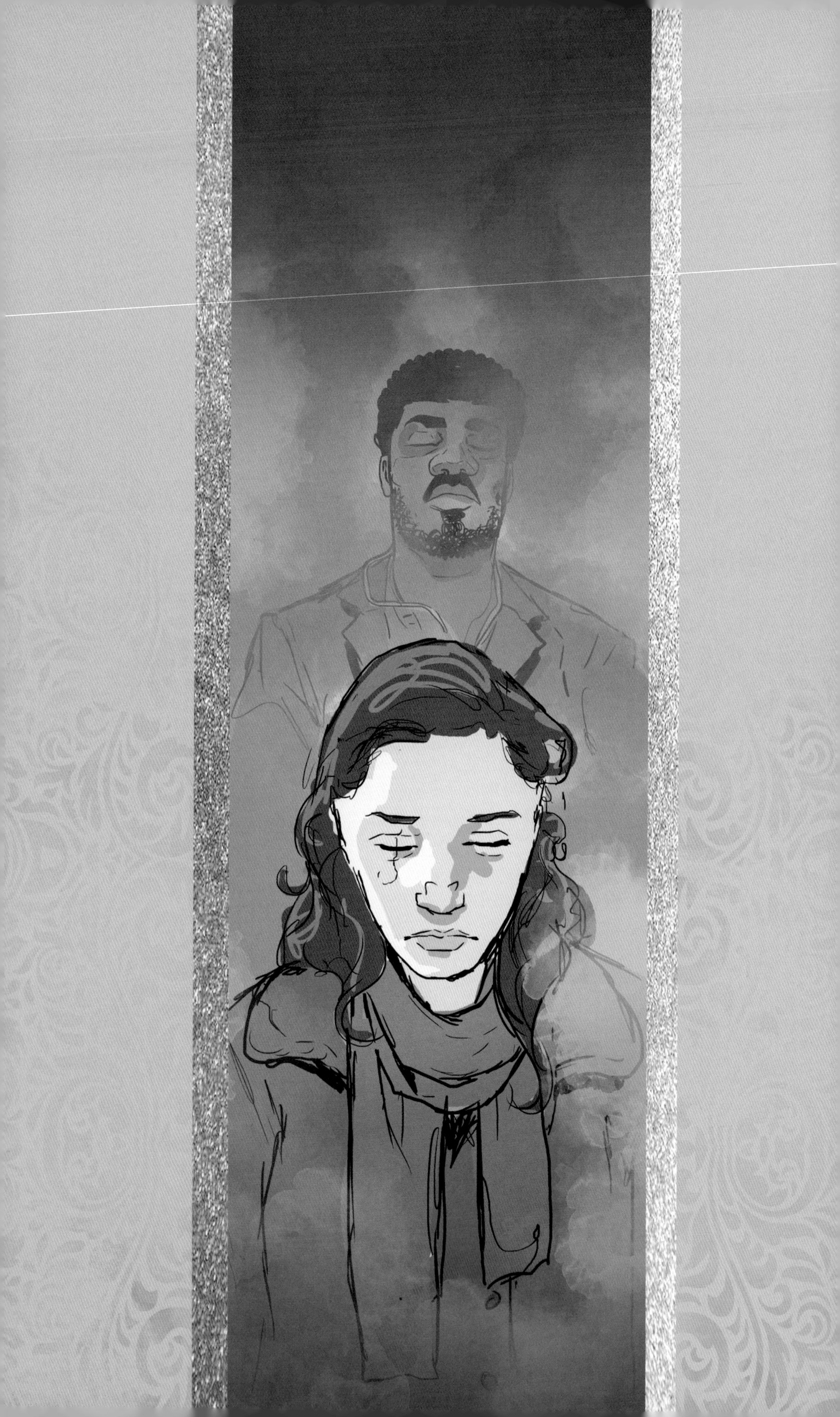

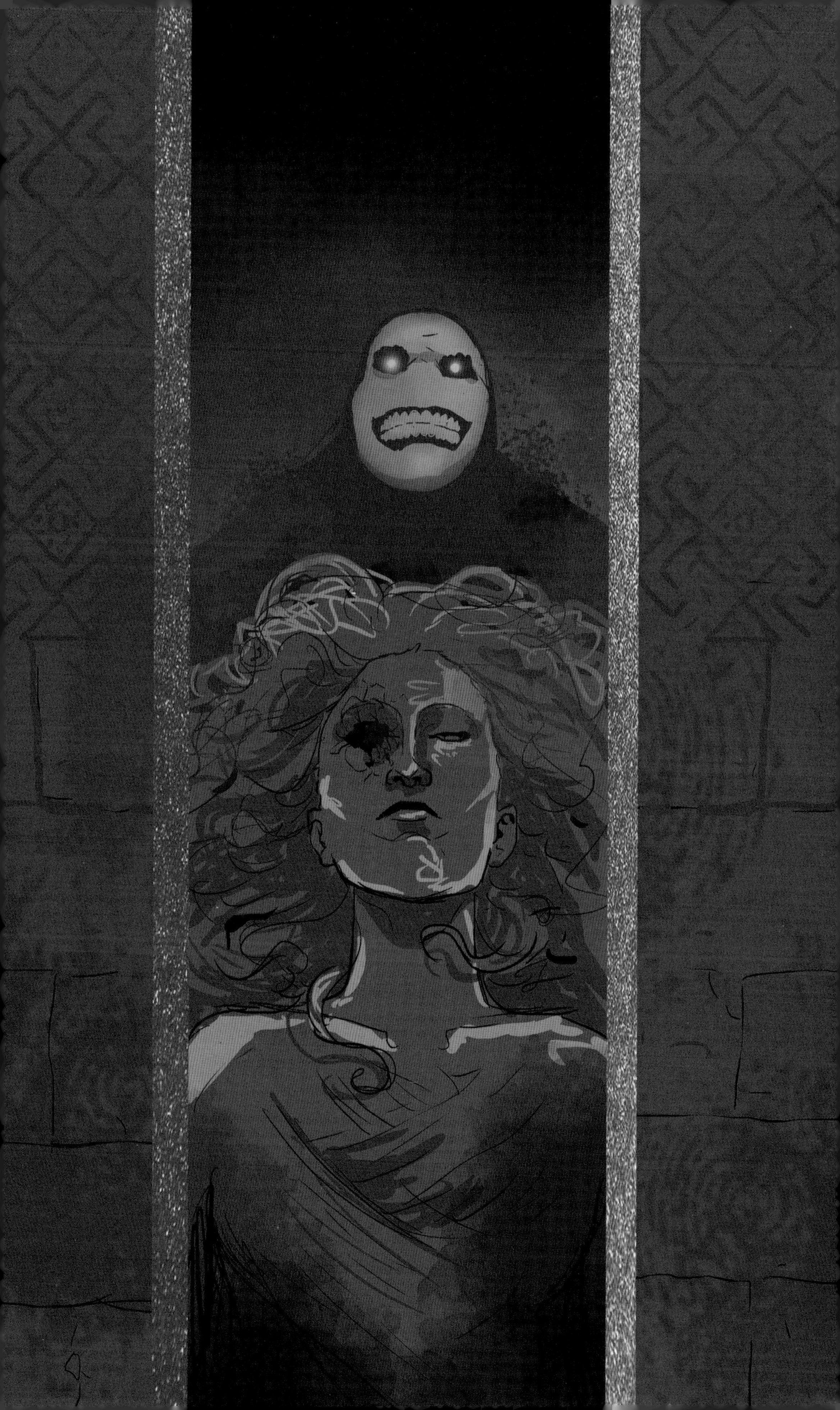

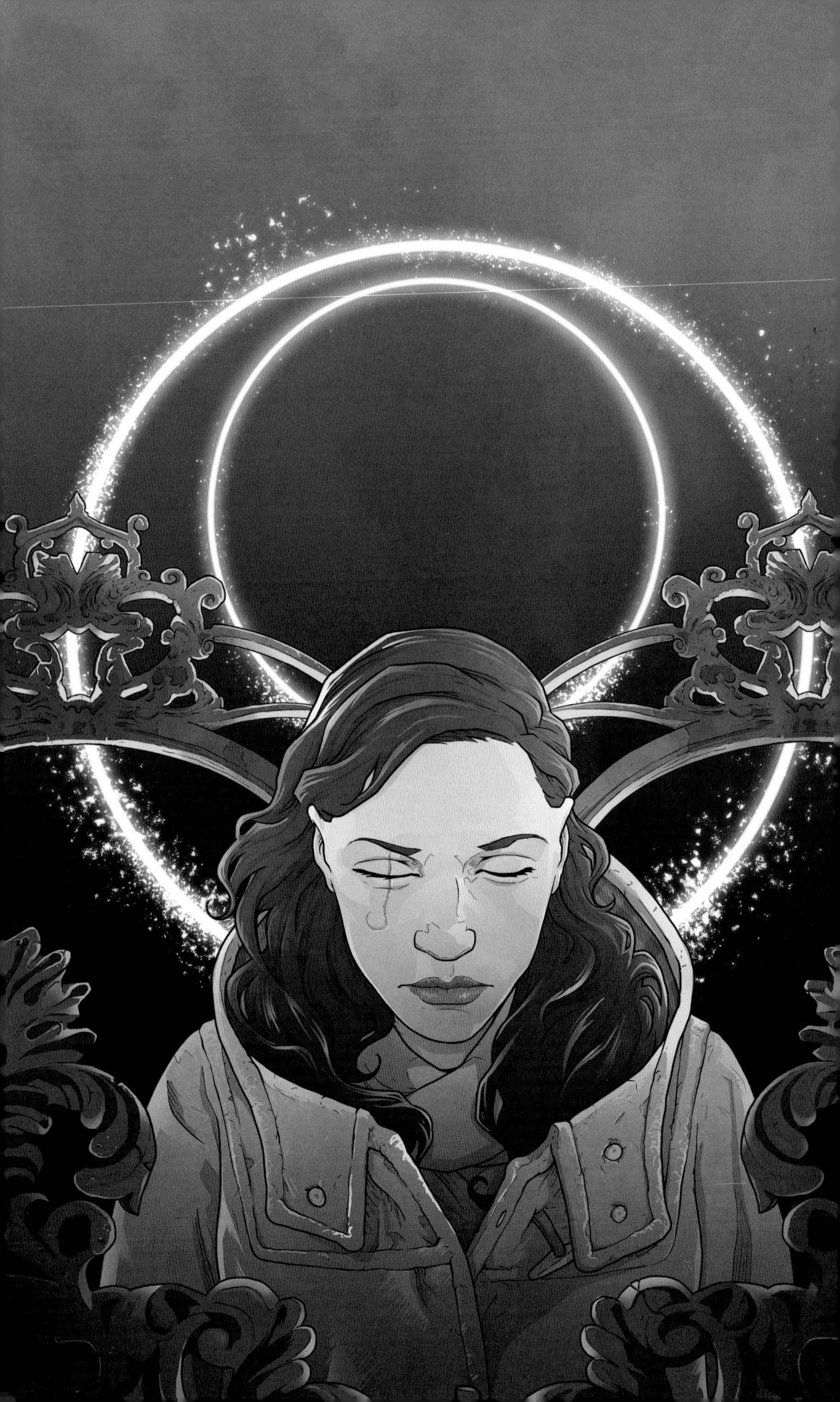

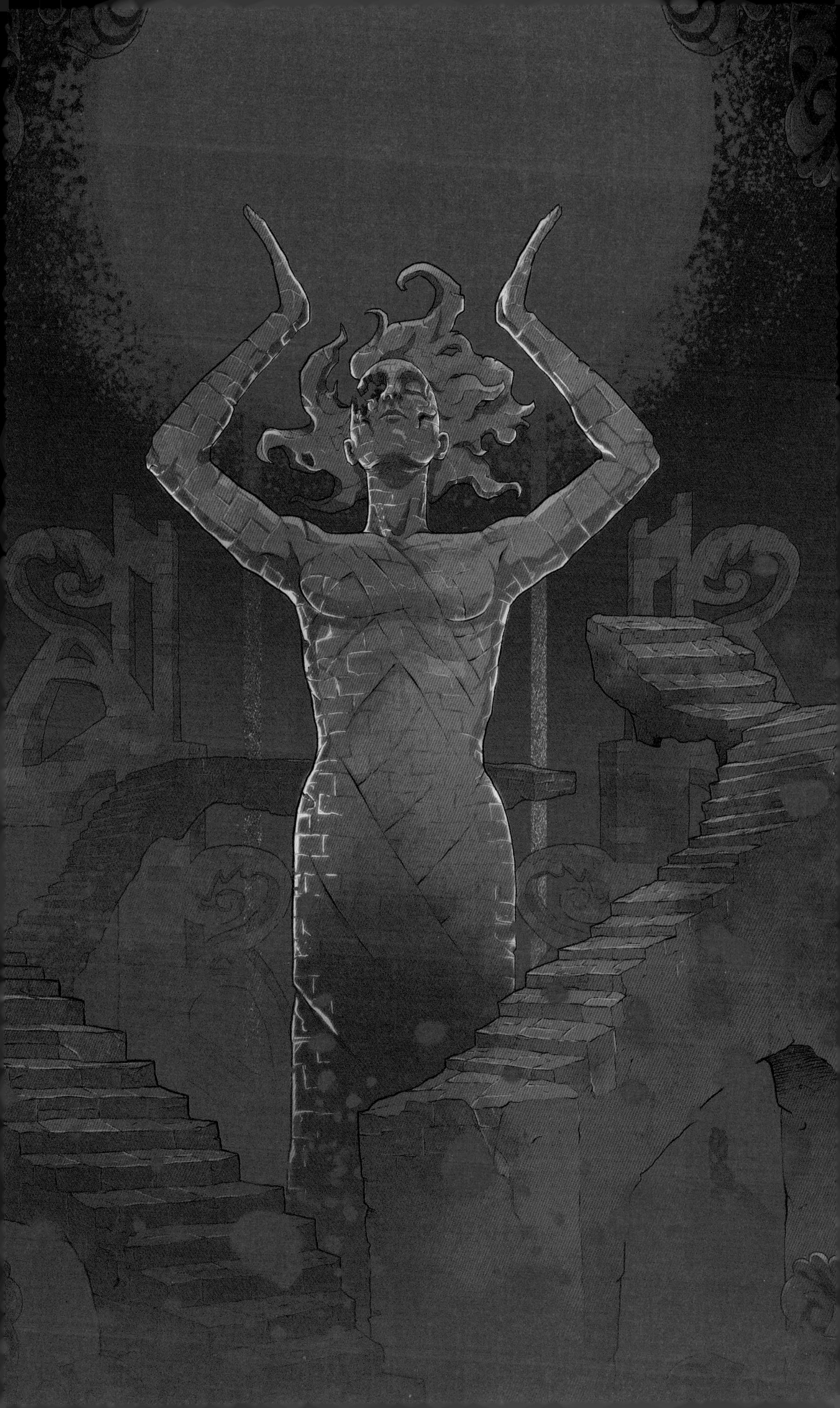

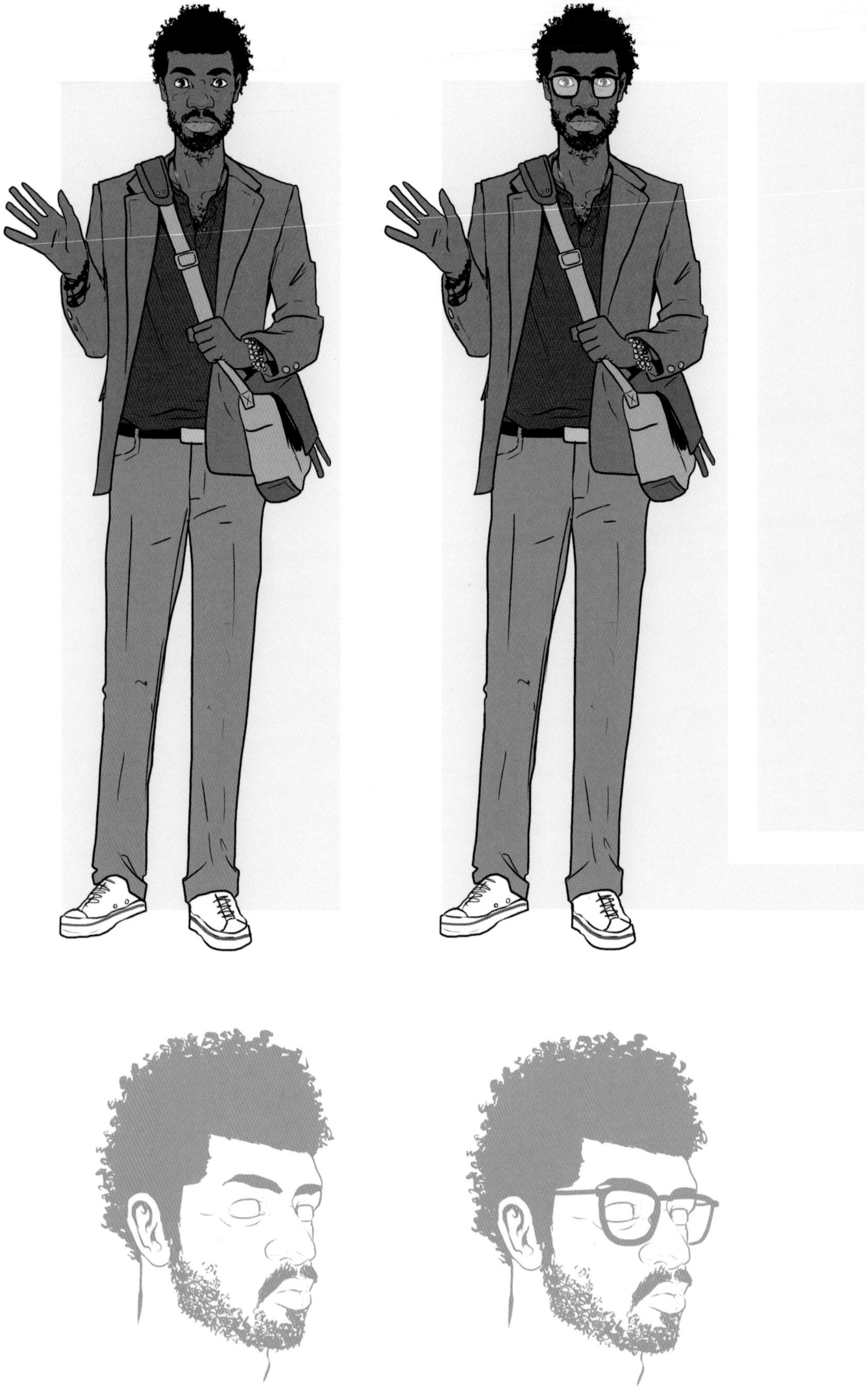

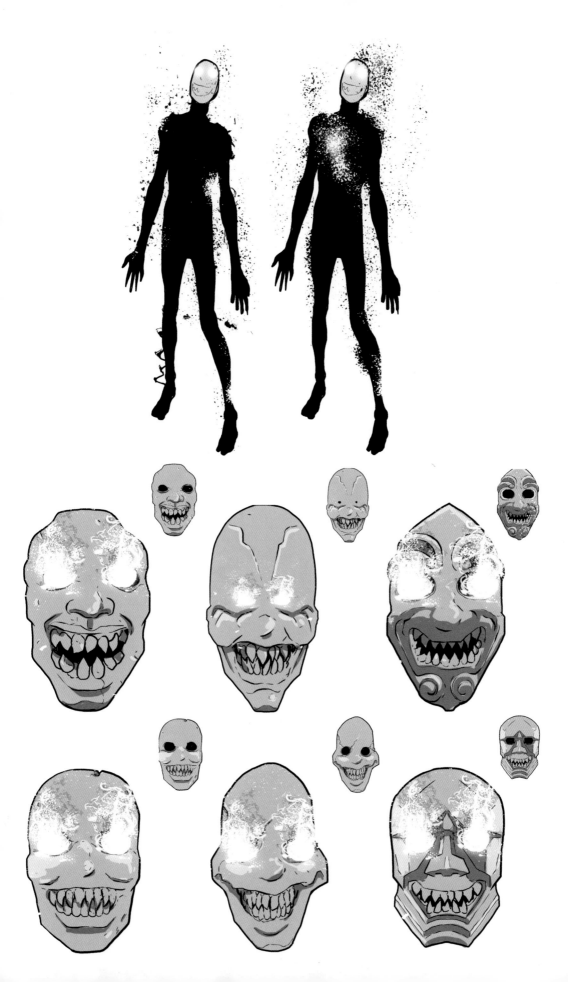

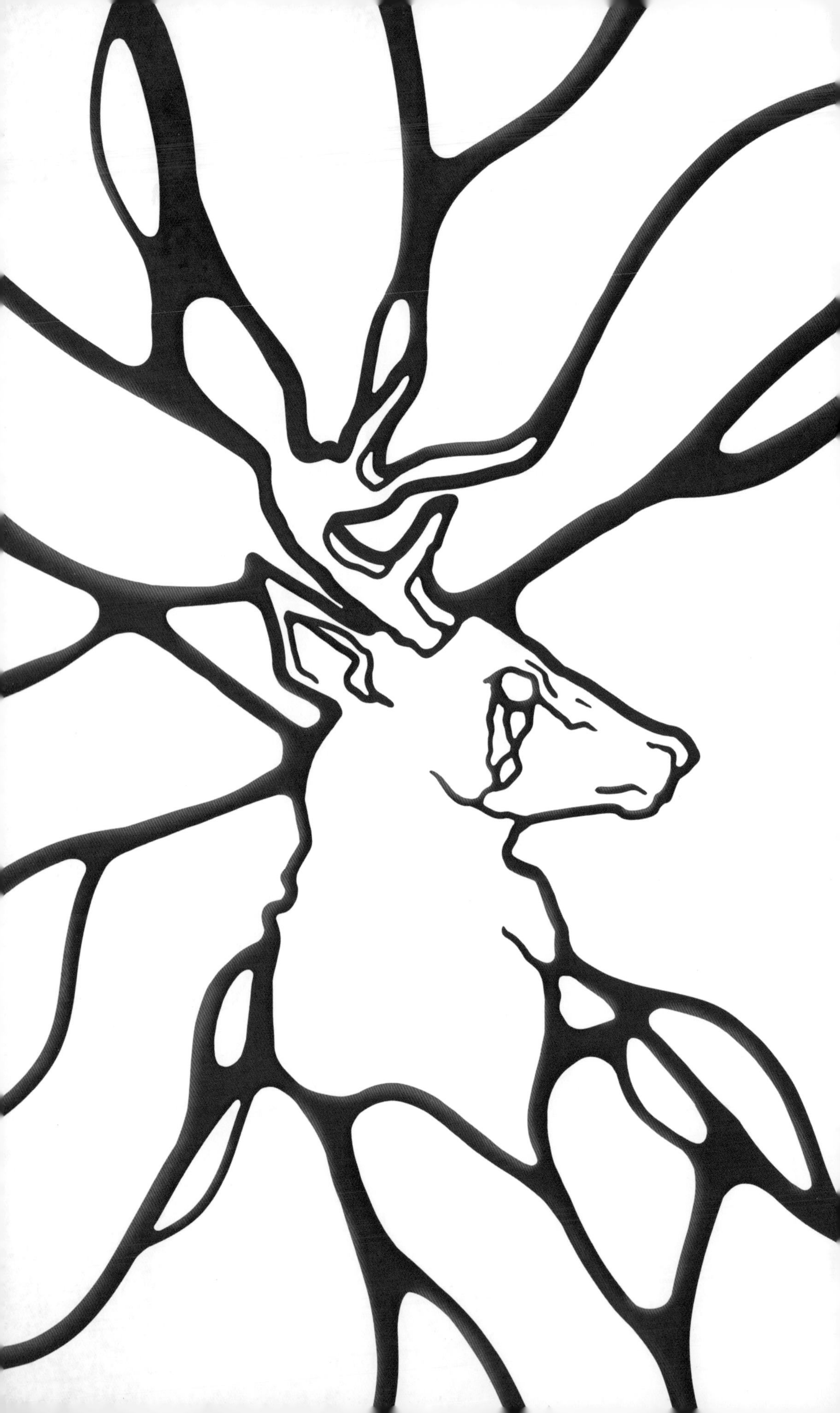

JEREMY HAUN is the creator and artist for *The Realm* from Image Comics. He is also the writer and occasional artist for acclaimed series *The Beauty* from Image Comics. Haun has worked on *Batwoman*, *Constantine*, and *Wolf Moon* with DC Comics, *RWBY* with Viz Media, *Iron Man: Civil War* with Marvel Comics, *The Darkness* with Top Cow, and more.

DANNY LUCKERT studied illustration and cartooning at the School of Visual Arts in NYC and upon graduating, Luckert immediately went to work in the comic book industry. He has worked on several miniseries with Red 5 Comics, such as *Haunted* Vol. 1 & 2 and *Riptide* Vol. 1 & 2. Luckert has also worked on *Tethered* with writer/co-creator David Pretch, as well as *Regression* with writer Cullen Bunn and colorist Marie Enger from Image Comics.

Born in Seoul, Korea, **ED DUKESHIRE** is a graphic artist and Harvey-nominated comic book letterer who has worked in the biz since 2001. He has lettered titles from mainstream to creator-owned favorites. He also owns and operates the Digital Webbing website, a gathering place for comic creators. And you may even catch him playing video games once in a while.

DISCOVER
VISIONARY CREATORS

KIERON GILLEN DAN MORA
TAMRA BONVILLAIN
ONCE & FUTURE
VOLUME ONE
THE KING IS UNDEAD

JAMES TYNION IV
WERTHER DELL'EDERA
MIQUEL MUERTO
SOMETHING is KILLING the CHILDREN
VOLUME ONE
SCOTT SNYDER

Brian Azzarello · Maria Llovet
FAITHLESS

GRANT MORRISON
DAN MORA
Klaus
How Santa Claus Began

SIMON SPURRIER × MATÍAS BERGARA
CODA
VOLUME ONE
"This one is really special!"
—JEFF LEMIRE

matt kindt
tyler jenkins
GRASS KINGS
volume one

BOOM! STUDIOS™

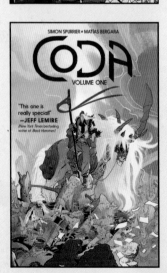

AVAILABLE AT YOUR LOCAL COMICS SHOP AND BOOKSTORE

To find a comics shop in your area, visit www.comicshoplocator.com

WWW.**BOOM-STUDIOS**.COM

Once & Future
Kieron Gillen, Dan Mora
Volume 1
ISBN: 978-1-68415-491-3 | $16.99 US

Something is Killing the Children
James Tynion IV, Werther Dell'Edera
Volume 1
ISBN: 978-1-68415-558-3 | $14.99 US

Faithless
Brian Azzarello, Maria Llovet
ISBN: 978-1-68415-432-6 | $17.99 US

Klaus
Grant Morrison, Dan Mora
Klaus: How Santa Claus Began SC
ISBN: 978-1-68415-393-0 | $15.99 US
Klaus: The New Adventures of Santa Claus HC
ISBN: 978-1-68415-666-5 | $17.99 US

Coda
Simon Spurrier, Matias Bergara
Volume 1
ISBN: 978-1-68415-321-3 | $14.99 US
Volume 2
ISBN: 978-1-68415-369-5 | $14.99 US
Volume 3
ISBN: 978-1-68415-429-6 | $14.99 US

Grass Kings
Matt Kindt, Tyler Jenkins
Volume 1
ISBN: 978-1-64144-362-3 | $17.99 US
Volume 2
ISBN: 978-1-64144-557-3 | $17.99 US
Volume 3
ISBN: 978-1-64144-650-1 | $17.99 US

Bone Parish
Cullen Bunn, Jonas Scharf
Volume 1
ISBN: 978-1-64144-337-1 | $14.99 US
Volume 2
ISBN: 978-1-64144-542-9 | $14.99 US
Volume 3
ISBN: 978-1-64144-543-6 | $14.99 US

Ronin Island
Greg Pak, Giannis Milonogiannis
Volume 1
ISBN: 978-1-64144-576-4 | $14.99 US
Volume 2
ISBN: 978-1-64144-723-2 | $14.99 US
Volume 3
ISBN: 978-1-64668-035-1 | $14.99 US

Victor LaValle's Destroyer
Victor LaValle, Dietrich Smith
ISBN: 978-1-61398-732-2 | $19.99 US